Weaponization of Ignorance

How Lies and Misinformation Divided America

Stephen M. Fry, Ph.D.

SBDI Publishing
www.SBDIPublishing.com

Weaponization of Ignorance:

How Lies and Misinformation Divided America

By Stephen M. Fry, Ph.D.

*Published by **SBDI Publishing***
El Dorado Hills, California

ISBN: 978-0-9858286-5-3

Cover design by SBDI Publishing

Interior design and formatting by the author

Printed in the United States of America
First Edition

For more information, visit: SBDIPublishing.com

Table of Contents

"Ignorance is the root and stem of all evil."
Plato

"The truth is still the truth, even if no one believes it.
A lie is still a lie, even if everyone believes it."
David Stevens

"It's easier to fool people than to convince them that they
have been fooled."
Mark Twain

Preface

No, I am not the famous British comedian and writer Stephen Fry (though British Airways often treats me as if I were). I am, instead, an average American citizen who, over the past decade, has become deeply concerned about the future of the United States. This isn't just a political concern—it's a civic one, with implications for how we raise children, educate students, and preserve democratic values for future generations.

It still astonishes me that nearly half the electorate accepted Trump's lies and overlooked his deeply flawed character—enough to vote for him. But a second time? Like many Americans—and stunned observers around the world—I've been both surprised and disturbed not only by Trump himself, but by the millions who appear gripped by a cult-like devotion to him.

I've spent countless hours wondering how friends, neighbors—even family members—came to believe obvious lies. More broadly, I've been unsettled by the growing number of people who embrace disinformation, conspiracy theories, and outright falsehoods.

Even more troubling has been the widespread erosion of trust in science, expertise, and the institutions responsible for educating and informing the public. How can flat Earth beliefs still persist in an age of GPS, sophisticated electronics, space flight, and instant access to the world's knowledge? If even basic truths about science, history, and governance become politically disputed, how can educators fulfill their mission—or parents prepare their children to be thoughtful citizens?

My initial, naïve assumption was that people simply weren't receiving the same information—and that, once exposed to facts, their intelligence and logic would naturally lead them to rational conclusions. I blamed much of the problem on Fox News, and wondered how smart viewers could believe blatant lies when even a brief glance at other networks might change their minds.

But I was wrong. While I'm not an academic in psychology or political science, I immersed myself in the growing body of literature on misinformation, political belief, and cognitive bias. I learned that a combination of psychological vulnerabilities, strategic disinformation, and a fragmented media ecosystem—amplified by filter bubbles and echo chambers—has enabled large-scale deception. And far beyond partisan squabbles or policy disagreements, this deception has already eroded key foundations of democracy and threatens to push the country toward authoritarianism.

Many popular books offered valuable insights into different aspects of the problem. David Corn's *American Psychosis* helped trace the evolution of the Republican Party. Anna Merlan's *Republic of Lies* cataloged many of the conspiracy theories of the past decade. Ezra Klein's *Why We're Polarized* explored how political identities drive polarization. Tom Nichols' *The Death of Expertise* described a nation "obsessed with the worship of its own ignorance." In *Ministry of Truth*, Steve Benen shows how the Republican Party has waged a campaign to rewrite recent history—seeding alternative narratives and suppressing inconvenient facts.

Jonathan Rauch's *The Constitution of Knowledge* outlined how liberal societies create and maintain truth—and how this infrastructure is under threat. Jason Stanley's *How Fascism Works* lays bare the mechanisms that authoritarian leaders use to manipulate truth, vilify opponents, and consolidate power. And Steven Levitsky and Daniel Ziblatt's *How Democracies Die*, written during Trump's first term, identified many of his actions as authoritarian and questioned whether democracy could endure. Two books by Brian Stelter—*Network of Lies* and *Hoax*—documented how Fox News colluded with Trump in ways that have deeply damaged American democracy.

One of the most comprehensive and compelling books I read was Barbara McQuade's *Attack from Within*, a powerful, meticulously sourced analysis of how disinformation threatens democracy and the rule of law. Yet despite its impressive scope—supported by more than 1,700 references—only one chapter addressed the core question that preoccupied me: Why do intelligent people fall for lies and conspiracy theories?

While these books deepened my understanding and framed many aspects of the crisis, I realized there was still something missing—a concise, accessible guide that didn't just catalog disinformation, but explained the psychological, social, and media-driven mechanisms that make it so powerful, so persistent, and so hard to dislodge. Most works focused on outcomes, patterns, or political actors; few examined *why otherwise intelligent people come to believe obvious falsehoods*—or how to reach those caught in that trap. That gap in the conversation became the driving force behind this book.

I had been thinking about writing something—especially if it might change minds—for nearly a decade; after Trump was out of office, the project seemed less urgent. But everything changed in 2025. The danger is no longer hypothetical—it is unfolding in front of us, every day.

Trump's second term has moved far beyond populist rhetoric and into authoritarian governance. He has opened federal investigations into media outlets critical of him, proposed defunding PBS and NPR, blocked the Associated Press from White House briefings, and filed lawsuits against journalists and publishers. Loyalists have replaced career civil servants in the National Archives, ensuring that the public record reflects his narrative—not necessarily the truth. These are not isolated actions—they follow a clear pattern drawn straight from the autocratic playbook.

Trump has also worked to eliminate institutional oversight. Inspectors General and independent watchdogs have been removed or sidelined. Executive Orders are being issued at a staggering pace, many later ruled unconstitutional—but the damage is often done before courts can intervene. Simultaneously, Fox News and other pro-Trump media outlets shield their audiences from these realities, creating a parallel world in which Trump's unchecked authority goes virtually unchallenged. Truth itself is being rewritten in real time, and the tools we once relied on—press freedom, independent agencies, even constitutional checks—are being hollowed out.

Those developments re-motivated my efforts to address the problem—but they also forced a shift in focus. My original goal was to reach those who had been deceived—particularly members of the Trump base who might still be open to reconsidering their beliefs. But through both research and direct efforts to communicate across ideological divides, I came to understand just how deeply misinformation becomes entrenched. It became clear that I could not persuade those who had become embedded in a cult-like culture—one actively shaped and reinforced by their media environment.

Therefore, the goal of this book is not to change hardened minds. Instead, it offers a framework for understanding how and why people become ignorant of political facts—and why they resist change even when confronted with evidence. To fulfill that goal, the book must be honest about where disinformation is most concentrated and consequential.

While disinformation exists across the political spectrum, this book focuses primarily on the right—not because the left is blameless, but because the scale, coordination, and real-world consequences of falsehoods originating from the political right are fundamentally different.

Media outlets on the left have their own biases and blind spots, and they are not above framing or selective emphasis. But most still operate within the norms of responsible journalism—issuing corrections, relying on evidence, and striving for factual accuracy.

In contrast, Right-wing disinformation campaigns—fueled by partisan media, social media influencers, and political leaders—have promoted provably false claims even after legal rulings and fact-checks, and have done so in ways that are pervasive, deliberate, and resistant to correction. These falsehoods have not just misled audiences—they have eroded democratic institutions, fomented political violence, and created a parallel reality immune to evidence.

The disinformation crisis threatening American democracy is not a "both sides" problem. It is an asymmetrical assault on truth that demands clear-eyed analysis, not false equivalence.

Weaponization of Ignorance examines how the modern American Right has weaponized cognitive vulnerabilities and media fragmentation to entrench ignorance and erode democratic norms. It isn't a scholarly treatise, but rather a handbook for fact-based individuals seeking to better understand their "across-the-aisle" friends, neighbors, and family members. It aims to help readers navigate and engage more productively in a society increasingly divided by weaponized ignorance.

I hope it motivates others to do their part in protecting truth—and defending the democratic values that depend on it.

Introduction

I used to believe that intelligence and knowledge naturally led people toward rational conclusions. I assumed that if individuals were presented with the same facts, they would at least agree on reality—even if they drew different conclusions from it. That belief has steadily unraveled.

Some of the most accomplished people I know—scientists, physicians, engineers—have become unwavering supporters of Donald Trump and the MAGA movement. These are individuals trained in logic, evidence evaluation, and critical thinking. And yet, they have embraced obvious falsehoods, rejected verified evidence, and repeated conspiracy theories that disintegrate under even mild scrutiny. I had to confront a difficult truth: intelligence alone offers no immunity against political ignorance.

This pattern isn't isolated. Across the country, millions of Americans—including many with advanced degrees and impressive credentials—have succumbed to disinformation. They dismiss mainstream journalism as "fake news," accept Trump's word over sworn testimony, and believe that only a handful of partisan outlets can be trusted. At the same time, they ignore the overwhelming international consensus reported by organizations like the BBC, Reuters, and NHK.

For many, truth has become tribal—and reality, optional. If only a handful of partisan outlets are to be trusted, while virtually all international and mainstream news organizations are dismissed as corrupt or conspiratorial, then what remains is not healthy skepticism, but the belief that nearly the entire global press is part of a coordinated deception.

This detachment from shared facts has not emerged by accident. It has been cultivated—carefully and deliberately—through an evolving ecosystem of propaganda, Right-wing media, algorithmic amplification, and political strategy. Trump's attacks on the press were not rhetorical flair; they were an opening move in dismantling the infrastructure of public knowledge. In its place, a parallel information system has taken root—one in which loyalty outranks logic, and truth is whatever the leader declares. These shifts don't just affect political debates—they impact classrooms, newsrooms, and dinner tables, eroding our collective ability to agree on reality itself.

How did this happen? How can rational people remain devoted to beliefs so clearly contradicted by evidence?

The answer is ignorance—but not the simple absence of knowledge. This is a more insidious form: ignorance that is manufactured, sustained, and weaponized. It thrives on repetition, identity reinforcement, and insulation from dissonant facts. It is not the result of accidental misinformation—it is the product of a system designed to deceive.

We have watched this unfold in real time. Consider the events that should have been political turning points: the Mueller Report, two presidential impeachments, the January 6 insurrection and its aftermath, the Dominion lawsuit against Fox News, and the rise of Project 2025. These are not fringe stories. They are central to the functioning of American democracy. And yet millions remain unaware—or worse, believe the opposite—of what actually occurred.

This ignorance is chosen, curated, and reinforced. In today's fragmented media environment, remaining uninformed takes effort: avoiding credible sources, rationalizing contradictions, and distrusting any evidence that threatens one's identity. For many, that effort has become routine.

This book is about the forces that make such ignorance possible—and the ways those forces are used to control public perception. It explores the psychological roots of belief, the media tactics that entrench disinformation, and the social dynamics that transform falsehood into loyalty. It shows how political operatives, media figures, and authoritarian leaders exploit these vulnerabilities—not to persuade, but to dominate the narrative.

You don't have to be gullible to fall into this trap. You just have to prioritize identity and emotional certainty over truth and uncomfortable reality.

In the chapters ahead, we explore how disinformation spreads, why it endures, and how it has reshaped American political life. **Part One** examines the psychological and cognitive mechanisms that make people vulnerable to falsehoods, including bias, tribalism, and conspiratorial thinking. **Part Two** looks beyond deception itself to understand the deeper appeal—why so many Americans, particularly on the political right, have become receptive to disinformation, drawing on history, identity, and moral frameworks. **Part Three** analyzes how Donald Trump and his allies deliberately exploited these dynamics, using media manipulation and narrative control to foster loyalty, suppress dissent, and dismantle democratic norms. Finally, **Part Four** offers a path forward: strategies for cultivating critical thinking, promoting media literacy, and engaging productively with those caught in misinformation—along with broader reforms to help restore a shared commitment to truth.

This book is not an attack on those who hold different political views. It is an attempt to understand why so many people believe things that are simply not true—and why those beliefs prove so resistant to correction. It offers tools for identifying disinformation, strategies for responding to it, and ideas for renewing a democratic culture grounded in facts.

The war on truth is real. And in 2025, it has intensified. If we fail to understand and counter the systems that weaponize ignorance, we risk losing not just the next election—but the very foundation of democracy itself. And it's not just an American crisis—around the world, authoritarian movements are watching, learning, and replicating these same tactics to undermine shared truth.

Part One: The Foundations of Political Ignorance

Ignorance in today's society is not simply the absence of knowledge—it is often carefully shaped through emotion, repetition, and tribal loyalty. While we like to believe that people form opinions based on facts and reason, the truth is more complicated. Beliefs are shaped by the stories we hear, the emotions we feel, and the communities we identify with. These influences are not always benign. In many cases, they are actively manipulated.

Ignorance is now cultivated—not just by fringe groups or bad actors, but by powerful media systems, political operatives, and social platforms that profit from outrage, division, and blind allegiance. The goal is not merely to misinform, but to reshape perception: to make people doubt what is real, trust what is false, and remain loyal even when the facts fall apart.

Part One lays the groundwork for understanding how this happens. It explores the psychological, emotional, and structural foundations of political ignorance—how misinformation becomes believable, why falsehoods spread faster than facts, and what draws ordinary people into closed systems of belief.

These chapters explain *why* certain beliefs take hold, even when they seem irrational or factually indefensible from the outside.

Part One examines:

- The cognitive and emotional roots of misinformation acceptance
- How repetition, emotion, and media amplify falsehoods
- The role of echo chambers and algorithmic curation in distorting reality
- How conspiracy theories thrive by satisfying psychological needs for control, clarity, and community
- How political tribalism evolves into loyalty, extremism, and even cult-like behavior

By understanding these mechanisms, we can better recognize the architecture of today's disinformation ecosystem. We are not simply witnessing political disagreement—we are facing a deliberate assault on shared reality.

Part Two shifts focus from *how* misinformation spreads to *why* so many people support political movements that rely on it. Not all Republican voters are misled; many are driven by economic self-interest, cultural tradition, or deeply held moral and religious values. Others are motivated by a sense of grievance or identity. This next Part explores those varied motivations, recognizing that not all support for extremist politics is rooted in ignorance or deception.

Chapter 1

The Cognitive Roots of Misinformation

Before we explore how lies spread, why the media distorts truth, or how political movements manipulate public perception, we must understand something even more fundamental: how people come to believe anything at all.

Beliefs rarely emerge from cold logic or objective analysis. More often, they take shape through emotion and identity, guided by unconscious mental shortcuts[1]. These psychological tendencies—like confirmation bias and motivated reasoning—affect both the content of people's beliefs and the way those beliefs are formed. And in an age of polarization, misinformation, and tribal politics, understanding these mechanisms is essential to making sense of political ignorance.

This chapter introduces the key psychological patterns that will appear throughout the book. Recognizing these cognitive traps can help us resist manipulation and open the door to more honest dialogue, even in a media landscape designed to mislead.

Defining Terms

The term **ignorance**, for purposes of this book, is defined as a lack of knowledge, awareness, or understanding. Although often used pejoratively, to imply a lack of education, ignorance may also be *willful*—when an individual chooses not to learn or understand—or it may be manipulated by external influencers, which is our primary concern.

Political ignorance may involve a lack of awareness of key political events or a false portrayal of events by manipulative actors—such as politicians or hyper-partisan news media. As Ilya Somin explains in *Democracy and Political Ignorance*[2], "When it comes to politics, ignorance is not just a failure of information. It's a systematic pattern—people don't know basic facts, and they don't even know what they don't know."

For example, if people have not read the Mueller Report but have only heard Bill Barr's interpretation (and its corroboration by Fox News), it can be argued that they are ignorant of what is actually contained in the report and its key findings. Although Barr's summary framed the report as exonerating Trump, later analysis—including the full text of the Mueller Report—revealed that his characterization was highly misleading and omitted key findings related to obstruction of justice.

While each side claims to have the "truth," and that the other side believes in "fake news," the situation is not symmetrical: there is only one truth. So-called "alternative facts" are, in our terminology, lies and misinformation.

Misinformation is defined here as false or misleading information, regardless of how it was spread—whether accidentally, unintentionally, negligently, or purposefully. In this book, we use misinformation as a general term; if a person is "trapped in misinformation," it does not matter how the falsities were acquired.

Disinformation, on the other hand, is the subset of misinformation that is intentionally spread to deceive and manipulate public opinion. When we talk about a campaign to deceive, it—by definition—is a disinformation campaign. It is *disinformation* that is most concerning, because if people believe it, they have been purposely deceived. An important portion of this book attempts to describe why disinformation is believed and, often, becomes deeply entrenched.

Throughout this book, the term misinformation is used as the general term for false information, regardless of how obtained; and disinformation is reserved to identify the purposeful spread of untruths for political purposes.

Confirmation Bias and Motivated Reasoning

Confirmation bias is the tendency to seek out and accept information that supports what we already believe, while dismissing or discrediting evidence that contradicts it. Taber Lodge in *Motivated Skepticism*[3] says, "People are not open-minded processors of information but rather selectively credit or discredit information based on whether it supports their preexisting beliefs." This bias operates automatically and often unconsciously. It feels good to encounter validating information—it reinforces our sense of being right, while contradictory facts trigger discomfort or distrust.

In the digital age, confirmation bias is amplified by personalized newsfeeds, partisan media, and algorithm-driven content. Psychologist Ziva Kunda noted this dynamic in her landmark study on motivated reasoning[4]: "People are more likely to arrive at conclusions they want to arrive at," because emotion often guides cognition more than facts. A person convinced that the 2020 election was stolen, for instance, will naturally gravitate toward fringe websites, viral memes, and misleading videos that confirm this belief—while dismissing court rulings and bipartisan audits as part of a cover-up.

Motivated reasoning is closely related. It refers to our unconscious tendency to process information in a way that supports a desired conclusion, often to protect our identity or worldview. For example, someone emotionally invested in anti-vaccine ideology may seek out obscure studies to bolster their skepticism while dismissing more robust scientific consensus. Instead of seeking truth, the mind works subtly to defend what it already believes. As Brendan Nyhan and Jason Reifler observed in their study of misperceptions[5], "People often resist factual information that challenges their preexisting views, even doubling down on the false belief."

These tendencies are especially dangerous in highly polarized environments, where partisan identity and media silos encourage individuals to reason not as truth-seekers, but as advocates. Even well-educated people fall prey to these biases when their core identities are at stake. According to Lilliana Mason in *Uncivil Agreement*[6], "Partisan identity is so powerful that people interpret facts differently depending on whether those facts help or hurt their party."

Cognitive Dissonance and Identity-Protective Cognition

Cognitive dissonance[7] is the discomfort we feel when we encounter information that conflicts with our beliefs or behavior. To reduce that discomfort, we often reinterpret reality. For example, a Trump supporter who believes in law and order but sees footage of the January 6th riot may rationalize the violence as justified, deny Trump's involvement, or shift blame to Antifa.

This rationalization becomes more pronounced when beliefs are tied to personal identity. **Identity-protective cognition** describes how we resist facts that threaten our social group or sense of self. For some Trump supporters, admitting that he lied or acted unlawfully would not merely be an intellectual concession, but a threat to their social and psychological identity.

In such cases, new facts are not just rejected—they are perceived as attacks. Political beliefs become tribal affiliations. Changing one's mind can feel like betrayal, not just of ideas, but of community.

The Dunning-Kruger Effect and Illusion of Understanding

The **Dunning-Kruger Effect** refers to the tendency of individuals with limited knowledge to overestimate their understanding. In politics, this means that people with the least expertise are often the most confident in their views. David Dunning described this in a 2011 study[8]: "The knowledge and intelligence that are required to be good at a task are often the same qualities needed to recognize competence—and without them, poor performers fail to see their own flaws."

Trump's appeal to "common sense" over expertise plays into this dynamic. His dismissal of scientific, military, and legal experts—paired with claims like "I alone can fix it" or "I know more than the generals"—resonated with followers who distrusted elites. For many, his confidence signaled truth, even when contradicted by evidence.

Many people hold strong opinions on immigration, taxation, or healthcare without being able to explain the underlying systems. They rely on talking points and headlines, mistaking familiarity for expertise. Psychologists Leonid Rozenblit and Frank Keil termed this the **"illusion of explanatory depth"**—the mistaken belief that we understand complex issues more deeply than we actually do[9]. This illusion is further compounded by the internet, where easy access to information inflates perceived understanding.[10]

The Availability Heuristic and Anchoring

The **availability heuristic** is a mental shortcut that leads people to judge the frequency or importance of an event based on how easily examples are recalled. For instance, after hearing repeated stories about voter fraud, people begin to assume it's widespread—even when data shows it's exceedingly rare. As Daniel Kahneman and Amos Tversky observed in their foundational work on cognitive heuristics[11], "People tend to assess the probability of an event by the ease with which instances come to mind." They continue, "A particularly salient example, even if rare, can lead to distorted estimates of frequency and risk."

This is exacerbated by media that spotlights sensational but atypical events. A single violent crime by an undocumented immigrant may dominate a news cycle and influence national policy, even though such crimes are statistically rare.

Anchoring, another cognitive shortcut, causes us to rely too heavily on the first piece of information we hear. If someone's first impression is that the election was stolen, all future evidence is evaluated through that initial frame. Early messaging creates a lens that colors everything else.

Social Proof, Echo Chambers, and Emotional Reasoning

Social proof is the tendency to assume that if many people believe something, it must be true. In online echo chambers, where users are surrounded by like-minded voices, this often creates the **illusion of consensus**. Seeing thousands of people echo a false claim can lend it undeserved credibility. Cass Sunstein explored this effect in *Republic: Divided Democracy in the Age of Social Media*[12], writing, "When like-minded people cluster, they reinforce each other's views, often becoming more extreme and more confident."

Social media algorithms intensify this by feeding users more of what they already believe. Over time, these tailored information streams form **ideological echo chambers**—self-reinforcing environments where dissent is filtered out and beliefs become more extreme.

Emotional reasoning adds fuel to the fire. People often believe things because they feel true. If a claim evokes anger, fear, or pride, it feels more real. Trump's rhetoric often leverages this by invoking emotional narratives of persecution, betrayal, or defiance. When belief is driven by feeling, facts struggle to break through. Psychologists Martel, Pennycook, and Rand found[13] that "Reliance on emotion promotes belief in fake news," as emotionally charged misinformation is more persuasive and more likely to be shared.

Why This Matters

None of these psychological patterns reflect stupidity. These mental shortcuts once helped us survive a complex world. Today, in the hands of media and politicians, they often work against us. Cultivating intellectual humility—recognizing the limits of one's own knowledge—can reduce defensiveness and foster openness to opposing views[14].

Understanding these mechanisms is essential to countering misinformation, polarization, and political manipulation. We cannot escape ignorance without first recognizing how our reasoning is shaped—often unconsciously—by emotion and identity. However, equipping people with critical thinking skills and media literacy has been shown to reduce their susceptibility to misinformation[15,16,17,18,19].

Beliefs may not always be rational. But understanding how they form is the first step in reclaiming them from those who seek to exploit them.

Yet forming a belief is only part of the story. Once established, false ideas are often reinforced through deliberate strategies designed to bypass reason and manipulate emotion. In the next chapter, we turn to the tactics used to entrench misinformation— particularly how repetition, emotional cues, and media systems can make even blatant falsehoods feel familiar, believable, and hard to dislodge.

Chapter 2

The Role of Misinformation in Shaping Beliefs

Misinformation can take many forms. Some is shared innocently—without fact-checking or malicious intent. *Disinformation* goes further. It's not accidental but strategic—carefully designed to mislead, provoke, and polarize.

This chapter explores how disinformation campaigns take advantage of repetition and emotion—and how they weaponize media systems to influence public perception, even when the facts are clear.

The Power of Repetition in Disinformation Campaigns

False narratives become entrenched when repeated frequently, especially by authority figures or trusted media sources. Psychological research has shown that people are more likely to believe something they hear multiple times, even if it is incorrect—a phenomenon known as the **illusory**

truth effect[1]. As Fazio and colleagues explain in their 2015 study in *Journal of Experimental Psychology*, "Repetition increases perceived truth, even when individuals know better."

Political messaging, propaganda, and social media all exploit repetition. Trump's continual insistence that the 2020 election was stolen—repeated through speeches, social media, and cable news—created a false consensus. In *Network Propaganda*[3], Benkler, Faris, and Roberts argue that "Fox News and the broader Right-wing media ecosystem constructed a self-reinforcing narrative around voter fraud, despite overwhelming evidence to the contrary." Despite audits and court rulings refuting the claim, its constant repetition gave it the appearance of truth.

Repetition also reinforces conspiracy theories. The more a claim is echoed across platforms, the more credible it appears. Flaxman, Goel, and Rao found[4] in their study on online media behavior that "users exposed to partisan content in digital echo chambers are more likely to mistake repetition for consensus." This "echo chamber effect" leads individuals to mistake coordinated messaging for independent confirmation. Repetition makes misinformation increasingly difficult to correct, as familiarity often overrides critical thinking.

Emotional Manipulation and Belief Reinforcement

Disinformation is engineered to provoke—and the emotions it targets most often are anger, fear, outrage, and resentment. These emotional reactions bypass rational filters, leading individuals to share or believe information before questioning its validity. We saw this dynamic during the COVID-19 pandemic, where misinformation about vaccines and public health measures spread rapidly, often fueled by emotion and distrust, as documented by Ball and Maxmen in *Nature*[5].

Take the anti-vaccine movement: misinformation is framed around fears of government overreach and loss of personal freedom. Similarly, political disinformation often exploits grievance-based narratives, such as fears of demographic change, cultural erosion, or economic instability.

Motivated reasoning, introduced in Chapter 1, is a cognitive bias that causes people to interpret emotionally resonant misinformation in ways that reinforce preexisting beliefs. Ziva Kunda, writing in *Psychological Bulletin*[6] (1990), observed that "Motivated reasoning allows people to arrive at conclusions they want to arrive at, justifying them with seemingly rational processes." Social media platforms further amplify this effect by boosting content that provokes strong emotional responses—regardless of its truthfulness. In this way, emotional manipulation deepens belief in false narratives and accelerates their spread.

Media and Political Amplification of Falsehoods

Misinformation spreads in predictable patterns, often led by political leaders, partisan media figures, and online influencers. These actors strategically promote falsehoods to deflect criticism, attack opponents, or mobilize political support.

For example, Trump's repeated claims of voter fraud were echoed by Fox News, Newsmax, and OANN, despite overwhelming evidence to the contrary. This created a layered media effect where disinformation was amplified across platforms, overwhelming fact-checkers and cementing false beliefs.

Even when false claims are debunked, they tend to leave a lasting imprint. Studies show that people tend to remember the original claim \ more than the correction. As Nyhan and Reifler demonstrated in their 2010 study on political misperceptions[7], "Corrections frequently fail to reduce misperceptions, and in some cases may even backfire." This makes **strategic deception**—a deliberate spread of misinformation—a powerful political tool.

Liberal media is not entirely immune. Even selective omissions or biased framing can subtly shape public understanding. However, the scale and coordination of Right-wing disinformation efforts—especially since 2016—have been far more pervasive and impactful.

Online influencers add another layer of amplification. With large audiences and minimal editorial oversight, they can rapidly disseminate falsehoods[8]. As Bakshy, Messing, and Adamic noted in their *Science* article[9] on Facebook's influence, "Information from friends—regardless of accuracy—has a strong effect on what people believe and share." They often position themselves as outsiders or truth-tellers, increasing their credibility among skeptical or disillusioned audiences.

Disinformation Campaigns in Action

Election Fraud Claims: Despite courts, audits, and bipartisan confirmations, Trump and Right-wing media repeatedly pushed the narrative that the 2020 election was stolen. This led directly to the January 6th insurrection[10].

Deep State Conspiracy Theories: The baseless idea that unelected bureaucrats secretly control the government has been used to justify attacks on institutions like the FBI and CDC[11,12,13].

COVID-19 Misinformation: Claims that the virus was a hoax or that vaccines contained microchips spread rapidly, undermining public health[5].

Cultural Grievance Campaigns: Issues like critical race theory or gender identity have been misrepresented and weaponized to inflame moral panic[14].

Immigrant "Caravans": Before elections, stories emerge of invading caravans heading for the border—narratives that quickly fade after ballots are cast[15].

In each case above, disinformation is not just incidental—it is strategic, and reinforced through repetition and emotional appeals. Recognizing these tactics is essential to building public resilience and protecting democratic discourse.

But disinformation doesn't spread in a vacuum. It thrives in a fractured media environment shaped by ideological silos, outrage-driven headlines, and algorithmic feedback loops that deepen division. The next chapter explores how this fragmented information landscape enables and accelerates the spread of falsehoods.

Chapter 3

Media Bubbles and Echo Chambers

Disinformation requires an ecosystem to thrive—and today's media environment provides it. The fragmentation of journalism has led to the rise of ideological silos, where individuals consume only the news that affirms their beliefs. This development has fundamentally altered how many people engage with information, creating echo chambers that amplify misinformation while crowding out dissent.

As media scholar Matthew Hindman noted in *The Myth of Digital Democracy*[1], "the fracturing of the media landscape has made it easier than ever to avoid political disagreement," accelerating ideological sorting and isolation.

The Evolution of Partisan Media

The shift toward media fragmentation did not happen overnight. In the past, major news networks like ABC, CBS, and NBC operated under the assumption of journalistic objectivity, offering relatively balanced

Examples of Journalistic Standards

- **Accuracy & Fact-Checking**—Ensure all reported information is accurate, verified, and supported by credible evidence.

- **Multiple Sources & Corroboration**—Verify claims with multiple independent sources before publishing.

- **Source Transparency**—Clearly identify sources whenever possible, explaining their relevance and potential biases.

- **Independence & Impartiality**—Avoid conflicts of interest and report news without personal, political, or financial bias.

- **Fairness & Balance**—Present multiple perspectives on controversial or complex issues.

- **Accountability & Corrections**—Promptly correct errors with clear retractions and explanations when mistakes are made.

- **Context & Proportionality**—Ensure that facts are presented with sufficient context and avoid giving fringe or extreme views equal weight.

- **Avoidance of Sensationalism**—Prioritize fact-based reporting over clickbait, exaggeration, or misleading headlines.

- **Minimizing Harm**—Report responsibly, considering the potential impact on individuals and communities.

- **Separation of News and Opinion**—Clearly differentiate factual reporting from editorial opinions, commentary, and analysis.

coverage that aimed to inform rather than persuade. But with the rise of cable television in the 1980s and 1990s, new players entered the scene—most notably CNN, which introduced the 24-hour news cycle. This marked the beginning of a more competitive and segmented media environment[2,3].

As competition intensified, networks began to differentiate themselves by appealing to niche audiences. Fox News, founded in 1996 by Roger Ailes and Rupert Murdoch, took a sharply conservative approach, branding itself as a counterweight to what it claimed was a liberal-leaning mainstream media[4]. Meanwhile, MSNBC positioned itself as a progressive alternative.

Over time, these shifts encouraged many media outlets to cater to specific ideological audiences, resulting in a gradual drift away from broadly accepted journalistic standards.

Traditional journalism prized objectivity and accuracy. Today's partisan outlets often emphasize loyalty and emotion over accuracy. For some networks, ideological narratives now take precedence over fact-based reporting, blurring the lines between journalism and entertainment.

Hyper-partisan media outlets often sidestep traditional journalistic standards. Controversy and emotional engagement generate higher ratings and revenue, so **outrage-driven** content has become the currency of modern newsrooms. According to Zeynep Tufekci in *Twitter and Tear Gas*[5], "attention is now the scarcest commodity online, and outrage is a dependable way to capture it," especially in politically charged news. Emotionally charged stories—especially on divisive issues like immigration and crime—tend to outperform objective reporting[6].

Conservative networks like Fox News have perfected this model, regularly presenting stories to heighten conservative grievances. Liberal networks are not immune, often highlighting threats from the political right and focusing heavily on inequality, civil rights, and the dangers of authoritarianism. The underlying strategy is the same—emphasize emotional reaction over dispassionate reporting[7].

This environment fosters **selective reporting**. Networks curate facts that support preferred narratives while omitting or downplaying those that might complicate the storyline. As documented by Jamieson and Cappella in *Echo Chamber*[8], "partisan media do not just offer slanted news—they alter the way audiences process political information." The result is a curated version of reality tailored to viewer expectations[9].

Over time, this dynamic conditions viewers to distrust opposing viewpoints. Political tribalism deepens, and audiences become entrenched in their media bubbles, where the "other side" is not just misinformed but dangerous. In *The Righteous Mind*[10], Jonathan Haidt writes, "once people join a political team, they get ensnared in its moral matrix," a mindset that discourages independent thought and casts dissent as disloyalty.

Hyper-partisan conservative outlets label mainstream journalism as "fake news," while liberal commentators dismiss Right-wing media as propaganda[11]. This reciprocal delegitimization erodes the possibility of shared understanding or dialogue.

The broader consequence is a public so divided by ideology that even basic facts become contested. Issues like climate change, public health, and election integrity are no longer debated on common ground— they're filtered through competing ideological lenses. The evolution of media from a shared civic forum to an echo chamber of partisanship has not only reshaped journalism but has undermined the informed citizenry that democracy depends on.

The Role of Social Media Algorithms

Social media platforms have become powerful reinforcers of ideological echo chambers, shaping the way individuals encounter and interpret information[12,13]. Unlike traditional media, which at least nominally adheres to journalistic standards, social media platforms operate on **engagement-driven algorithms**. These algorithms prioritize content that is most likely to keep users interacting— with likes, shares, comments—even if that content is divisive, misleading, or entirely false.

The logic is simple: the longer users stay on a platform, the more ads they see. And the best way to keep them engaged is to show them emotionally charged, attention-grabbing content—regardless of its accuracy.

Studies have shown that false information spreads faster than the truth. A 2018 MIT study published in *Science*[14] found that false stories on Twitter spread six times faster than factual ones, largely because misinformation is crafted to provoke emotional responses like outrage, fear, or amusement. The MIT researchers Vosoughi, Roy, and Aral found that "falsehoods were 70% more likely to be retweeted than the truth," attributing this to their novelty and emotional resonance.

These algorithms create filter bubbles—self-reinforcing information silos where users are fed a steady stream of content that aligns with their beliefs while being shielded from opposing views[15]. Someone who interacts with conservative-leaning posts, for example, will continue to receive more of the same. Over time, their feed becomes an echo chamber, insulating them from alternative perspectives.

The same mechanism drives radicalization. As reported by the Mozilla Foundation (Ribeiro, et.al. [16]) and supported by academic studies, YouTube's recommendation algorithm has repeatedly been shown to push users toward more extreme content in an effort to maximize engagement. As Zeynep Tufekci has noted[17], "[YouTube] may not start out with extremist content, but it knows how to serve it up with algorithmic precision." A person watching a video on border security might soon be fed anti-immigration conspiracies or white nationalist rhetoric—not necessarily because the platform promotes extremism, but because outrage sustains engagement.

Social media further amplifies confirmation bias—the tendency to favor information that supports preexisting beliefs. Individuals become more convinced of their views and increasingly dismissive of contrary evidence. Because these platforms tailor content to personal preferences, users begin to believe that their perspective is not just valid but universally obvious.

While some platforms have attempted to curb the spread of misinformation—through fact-checking, content removal, or downranking sensational posts— such efforts are often criticized by both sides. Conservatives accuse tech companies of censorship; liberals argue the platforms don't go far enough. These tensions make consistent, credible moderation difficult to achieve.

Ultimately, social media's design makes it a uniquely powerful vector for misinformation. Breaking its influence requires intentional behavior: seeking out varied sources, resisting knee-jerk engagement, and being open to complexity. Without such efforts, social media will continue to serve as an accelerant of division and disinformation.

The Decline of Local Journalism

Local journalism has long been a vital pillar of American democracy, providing accurate, community-based reporting that national outlets overlook. Yet over the past two decades, local journalism has collapsed. Thousands of newspapers have closed due to financial pressures, consolidations, and the rise of digital advertising.

As local newsrooms shutter, national outlets— often with ideological slants—fill the gap with generalized stories that don't reflect local conditions. The result is a widening disconnect between citizens and fact-based journalism. Local governance, school board decisions, and community policing go unreported, while national controversies dominate.

This shift has created **news deserts**—regions without meaningful local reporting. As Penny Abernathy, who coined the term "news deserts," has written[18], "The loss of local news is the loss of a community's watchdog, its curator of public debate, and its chronicler of daily life." Studies show that in such areas, political polarization intensifies and civic engagement declines[19]. People vote less, know less about local issues, and are more susceptible to national misinformation. Journalism scholar Robert McChesney emphasizes this[20], stating, "Without local journalism, we cannot have local democracy. Period."

In the absence of local journalism, partisan outlets shape local perception with broad, ideologically framed narratives. A national outlet may report a rise in crime, even if the local area is safe. Another may focus on systemic inequality while overlooking regions experiencing economic success. Without localized context, people absorb national narratives that may not reflect their communities at all.

Local journalism also plays a critical role in accountability. Investigative reports have historically uncovered corruption in city councils, school boards, and police departments. Without reporters asking hard questions, power goes unchecked. And when voters are uninformed about local policy or elections, civic participation suffers.

Efforts to revive local journalism—nonprofit models, public funding, or digital-first strategies—have shown some promise. Organizations like ProPublica's

Local Reporting Network have stepped in, but the reach and depth of traditional newspapers are difficult to replicate. Meanwhile, platforms like Facebook and Google have absorbed the advertising dollars that once sustained local papers.

Unless this decline is reversed, misinformation will continue to thrive in the absence of credible, localized reporting. Strengthening local journalism isn't just about preserving an industry—it's about preserving democracy where it begins: in our communities.

The Psychological Comfort of Echo Chambers

One reason echo chambers are so pervasive is that they feel good. When those around us share our views, it affirms our identity and reinforces our sense of safety. As Amanda Ripley explains in *The Atlantic*[21], "When we feel threatened, we don't see clearly. Our brains lock onto fight-or-flight mode, and we tend to seek protection inside our tribe—even if that means ignoring facts or turning against outsiders." This is confirmation bias in action—we welcome anything that reinforces our worldview—and instinctively push away what doesn't.

There's also cognitive dissonance, the mental discomfort we feel when confronted with conflicting information. Rather than revise our beliefs, we often rationalize or dismiss the new evidence. This can lead us to double down on false or extreme ideas, especially when changing our minds would be socially or emotionally difficult.

Social media deepens this dynamic by letting us curate our own informational environments. We unfollow, mute, or block dissenting voices, ensuring that our feeds remain comforting and ideologically pure. Over time, we may encounter opposing views less and less—not because they aren't out there, but because we've built a digital wall to keep them out.

This reinforces us-versus-them thinking. In extreme cases, opponents aren't merely wrong— they're cast as threats or enemies. Political movements and media networks exploit this division, portraying their side as righteous and the other as an existential threat.

Adding to this is the **backfire effect**, where people confronted with evidence that contradicts their beliefs actually become more entrenched. Instead of reassessing their views, they look for flaws in the opposing evidence or undermine the legitimacy of the source. As summarized[19] by political scientists Brendan Nyhan and Jason Reifler, "People who are misinformed often hold their beliefs with such strength that corrective information not only fails to change their minds—it actually makes them more certain they're right."

The consequences are serious. In a functioning democracy, people must be able to engage with differing viewpoints. But when individuals are locked inside echo chambers, political polarization worsens, shared facts disappear, and compromise becomes almost impossible.

In that vacuum of trust and shared reality, conspiracy theories flourish. They offer seductive explanations—scapegoats and secret plots—when truth feels uncertain or inconvenient. The next chapter explores why conspiracy thinking is so psychologically compelling—and how it becomes a powerful force in the absence of shared reality.

Chapter 4

The Psychology of Conspiracy Theories

Conspiracy theories have existed for centuries, but in the modern age, they've become more pervasive and politically potent. They offer deceptively simple answers to complex problems, often blaming powerful but hidden forces for society's ills.

While some begin with sincere doubt, many take root in emotional reasoning, social influence, and political ideology that lead people to reject reality in favor of emotionally satisfying alternative narratives.

Psychological Drivers of Conspiracy Thinking

Conspiracy theories thrive due to several psychological mechanisms that make individuals more susceptible to these beliefs. Confirmation bias is one of the most significant drivers—people naturally gravitate toward information that aligns with their preexisting beliefs while dismissing contradictory evidence. This is reinforced by motivated reasoning, where individuals actively seek out and interpret information in ways that confirm their worldview. For example, someone who distrusts the government may readily accept theories of government corruption, even when there's no credible proof.

Another key factor is the **need for control and certainty**. During times of crisis or instability, conspiracy theories provide a sense of order by offering a clear villain or explanation for otherwise confusing events. Research shows that when people feel powerless—whether due to economic struggles, political instability, or global upheaval—they are more likely to embrace narratives that assign blame to a specific group or entity. These theories act as coping mechanisms, offering psychological relief by attributing randomness or failure to deliberate actions. As psychologist Jan-Willem van Prooijen explains in *The Psychology of Conspiracy Theories*[1], "The need for certainty and control in the face of ambiguity or chaos often motivates people to adopt conspiracy beliefs, even when those beliefs are unfounded."

Fear and anxiety also play major roles. Anxious, overwhelmed individuals are more likely to adopt conspiracy thinking because these narratives provide comfort through structured explanations[2]. Believing in a conspiracy offers an illusion of control: a reason for the chaos, even if it's false. According to political scientist Joseph Uscinski in *Conspiracy Theories: A Primer*[3], "Conspiracy theories act as belief systems that help individuals make sense of a complex world, often by substituting intention for accident."

The Dunning-Kruger effect, introduced in Chapter 1, further contributes. People with limited knowledge often overestimate their understanding, believing they've found a truth that the experts—and most others—have overlooked. The internet reinforces this illusion by giving fringe theories and factual reporting equal visibility, blurring the line between expertise and speculation.

Social reinforcement strengthens these beliefs further. The more often someone encounters conspiracy-related content, through friends or fringe websites, the more credible the theory appears. This feedback loop is particularly strong within ideological communities, where external criticism is dismissed as part of the supposed conspiracy itself. As Katherine Olmsted notes in *Real Enemies: Conspiracy Theories and American Democracy*[4], "Conspiracy theories are not just explanations—they are tools for identity formation, shaping who people think they are and who they see as enemies."

The Social Aspect of Conspiracy Communities

Conspiracy theories rarely exist in isolation. They flourish in tight-knit communities where believers validate each other's views. In-group bias leads individuals to trust those within their ideological circle more than outside sources, even when those sources offer factual evidence[5]. This dynamic creates a powerful echo chamber in which alternative beliefs are actively dismissed.

One of the strongest reinforcements is the **need for belonging**. People seek out communities where they feel accepted and understood—especially when their views are fringe or controversial. Online platforms such as Reddit, Telegram, and private

Facebook groups make it easy to find others who share their perspectives, creating insular networks that shield members from outside scrutiny.

Members share articles, videos, and anecdotes that reinforce their views. Dissenting opinions are often rejected or ridiculed, while like-minded contributions are rewarded with affirmation. This self-reinforcing cycle makes it increasingly difficult for individuals to break away. Once inside, members often stay silent—not out of agreement, but fear of rejection. Those who question the group narrative may be labeled as traitors or accused of being "brainwashed" by mainstream media.

These groups also promote us-versus-them thinking, portraying outside sources—government officials, scientists, journalists, and even family members—as part of the conspiracy[6]. This **binary worldview** deepens loyalty, and feeds suspicion of anyone outside the group. In her 2023 book *Under the Influence*[7], journalist Kara Swisher observes, "Belonging to conspiracy communities offers a seductive sense of purpose and superiority. You're not just informed—you're initiated into a hidden truth." As a result, conspiracy believers often dismiss mainstream institutions entirely, seeing themselves as the enlightened few.

Crucially, conspiracy theories are **adaptive**. When faced with contradictory evidence, groups often reinterpret the facts rather than abandon the belief. Failed predictions are explained away, timelines are extended, and blame is shifted to new actors. For instance, when QAnon predictions about mass arrests didn't occur, believers claimed the "Deep State" had thwarted justice. This flexibility keeps conspiracy movements alive even when their foundational claims are disproven[8].

Because of this social entrenchment, combating conspiracy belief requires more than presenting facts. It also means addressing the emotional and social needs these groups fulfill. Offering nonjudgmental dialogue and alternative communities can help individuals detach without feeling isolated or attacked.

High-Profile Examples: QAnon, Election Fraud Theories, Anti-Vaccine Movements

Some of the most persistent conspiracy theories in recent years have had profound political and social consequences—shaping public discourse, influencing policies, and leading to violence[9].

One of the most notorious is **QAnon**, which began online in 2017. QAnon followers believe that a secret cabal of elites—including politicians, celebrities, and business leaders—is engaged in unspeakable crimes, and that Donald Trump was working behind the scenes to dismantle this hidden network. Despite a complete lack of evidence, QAnon gained widespread traction, infiltrated political institutions, and played a major role in mobilizing participants for the January 6th Capitol riot[10,11].

Another enduring example involves **election fraud claims** following the 2020 U.S. presidential election. Despite numerous audits, court decisions, and bipartisan confirmations affirming the election's legitimacy, millions continue to believe it was "stolen."

High-profile figures—including former President Trump—and conservative media outlets amplified this misinformation, leading to widespread mistrust of democratic processes and legislative changes to voting laws in several states[12].

The **anti-vaccine movement** has also been significantly driven by conspiracy thinking. False claims that vaccines contain microchips, alter human DNA, or serve a depopulation agenda circulated widely during the COVID-19 pandemic. These narratives fueled vaccine hesitancy, contributing to widespread and preventable illness and death. Medical studies[13,14] found a 43–76% higher COVID death rate among Republicans post-vaccine rollout, amounting to over 200,000 excess deaths—demonstrating the deadly toll of misinformation.

What makes these conspiracy theories particularly hard to dismantle is their resilience and adaptability. When predictions fail, followers often adjust the narrative rather than question its foundation. Timelines shift. Failed predictions are reinterpreted. And new justifications are always ready. This fluidity allows the movement to persist and continue recruiting new believers—even in the face of overwhelming disconfirmation.

The Resistance to Debunking and Corrective Information

A major challenge in addressing conspiracy thinking is the backfire effect. When presented with evidence disproving their beliefs, conspiracy theorists often double down. New information is interpreted as part of the conspiracy itself, not as grounds for reconsideration. As psychologist Stephan Lewandowsky writes in *Beyond Misinformation*[15], "Misinformation is sticky. People often continue to rely on false information even after a correction, especially when it aligns with their identity or worldview."

That's because conspiracy theories aren't just intellectual positions—they're tightly bound to identity, group belonging, and emotional investment. Believers often view themselves as brave truth-seekers who have seen through a widespread deception[16]. To abandon the theory means admitting they were misled, which feels like a personal failure or betrayal.

The phenomenon of cognitive dissonance—the discomfort caused by holding contradictory beliefs— adds another barrier. Rather than accept evidence that conflicts with their worldview, many rationalize or reinterpret the evidence to fit their existing framework. This preserves self-consistency, even when it requires increasingly implausible justifications.

Social media platforms complicate this further. Their algorithms serve emotionally engaging content—often conspiracy-related—because it drives clicks and keeps users online. Attempts to fact-check or label misinformation often backfire—further reinforcing conspiracy thinking. Many conspiracy believers claim that fact-checkers and journalists are themselves part of the deception, making traditional corrective methods ineffective[17].

Addressing these beliefs requires more than confrontation. Studies show that non-confrontational, open-ended conversations are more effective in promoting reconsideration[18]. Encouraging critical self-reflection, highlighting inconsistencies gently, and asking questions rather than giving lectures can slowly weaken the cognitive scaffolding of conspiracy belief.

Equally important is developing critical thinking skills and media literacy from a young age. People must learn how to evaluate claims, spot manipulation, and challenge their assumptions. Schools, libraries, and public institutions should make media education a core priority[19].

Without these systemic changes—both social and educational—conspiracy theories will continue to flourish[20]. They will shape political discourse, polarize communities, and erode the institutions that form the backbone of a functioning democracy[21].

For many, conspiracy thinking doesn't just shape belief—it defines who they are. In the next chapter, we explore how misinformation merges with identity, how loyalty overrides logic, and how political movements like Trumpism adopt cult-like characteristics that make facts almost irrelevant.

Chapter 5

The Dangers of Blind Tribalism and Cult-Like Behavior

Political identity has become central to how many people define themselves—making it difficult to change minds, even when the evidence is overwhelming. When truth comes into conflict with tribal loyalty, the facts often lose.

This chapter explores how political movements—especially Trumpism—can take on cult-like features, where allegiance to a leader or cause outweighs truth itself. While Trumpism is the clearest modern example, similar dynamics have appeared throughout history whenever ideology overtakes critical thinking[1].

The Psychological Mechanisms of Political Tribalism

Tribalism is an evolutionary trait that once helped humans survive by fostering cooperation within groups. In modern politics, this instinct can lead to fierce political loyalty—even when it undermines reason.

Groupthink compels individuals to conform to the beliefs of their in-group, even when those beliefs contradict evidence or personal values. As political psychologist Lilliana Mason explains in *Uncivil Agreement*[2], "Partisanship is not just about policy positions—it's about group identity, and that identity can override facts, norms, and even personal values." Because political beliefs are now deeply intertwined with personal identity, challenging someone's views often feels like a personal attack.

A major driver of tribal behavior is **social identity theory**, which suggests people derive a sense of self-worth from their group affiliations. This aligns with the original work[3] of Henri Tajfel and John Turner, who wrote, "The mere act of categorizing people into groups is sufficient to trigger in-group favoritism and out-group bias." When individuals strongly identify with a political party or movement, they often defend misinformation and reject opposing viewpoints as a way to protect their identity, not from misunderstanding, but from emotional dissonance.

One of Trump's political achievements has been the construction of the **MAGA** movement—named after his campaign slogan, *Make America Great Again*—which provides not only political direction but a sense of belonging. This cohesive identity has few parallels in modern American politics and helps explain the deep emotional investment of his base.

Cognitive dissonance further reinforces tribalism. As Leon Festinger, the originator of the theory, observed in *A Theory of Cognitive Dissonance*[4], "A person who experiences dissonance will actively avoid situations and information likely to increase it." When new information contradicts a strongly held belief, it creates discomfort. Individuals often explain the contradiction away, rather than reevaluate their position.

Motivated reasoning also plays a role. People process information in ways that confirm what they already believe while rejecting inconvenient facts[5]. In highly polarized environments—where issues are framed as battles between good and evil—this effect intensifies. The stronger the emotional investment, the harder it becomes to change one's mind.

Media fragmentation and social validation reinforce tribalism, where individuals selectively expose themselves to news that aligns with their ideology. Echo chambers filter out dissenting voices, while trusted insiders reinforce the dominant narrative. Outsiders offering corrective information are easily dismissed as biased or part of the problem.

Understanding these mechanisms is essential. To counter tribalism, we must create spaces where people can examine their beliefs without feeling socially threatened.

How Trumpism Mirrors Historical Cult Behaviors

Many analysts have noted that Trumpism shares characteristics with cult-like movements[6]. Cults are defined by absolute loyalty and deep distrust of anyone outside their inner circle. Trump's rhetoric reinforces this dynamic by positioning himself as the only person who can save the country from political and cultural ruin.

Supporters often show **apocalyptic thinking**—believing that without Trump, America faces existential collapse. This fear-driven loyalty ensures that criticism of Trump is seen not as valid dissent, but as a threat to the group itself.

Authoritarian leadership is a key cult trait. Trump has repeatedly dismissed oversight, scientific consensus, and critical reporting as conspiracies against him[7]. His followers often echo these claims, rejecting facts as "fake news" and accepting the leader's word— even when it flatly contradicts things he's said—or the facts on the ground.

Another hallmark is the **vilification of outsiders**. Trump routinely frames critics—including members of his own party—as traitors or un-American. This us-versus-them mentality encourages polarization and insulates the group from outside influence.

Trumpism also makes use of **thought-terminating clichés**—catchphrases like "Fake News," "Stop the Steal," and "Witch Hunt" that serve to shut down debate. Psychiatrist Robert Jay Lifton coined the term "thought-terminating cliché" to describe slogans that, as he wrote in *Thought Reform and the Psychology of Totalism*[8], "end the conversation by blocking further consideration." These phrases shut down discussion and signal allegiance to the cause.

While Trumpism doesn't isolate followers physically, it exhibits **informational isolation**. Supporters are told to distrust mainstream media, government agencies, and even friends or family members who challenge the movement. Eventually, this mistrust hardens into a self-contained worldview that facts can no longer penetrate.

Perhaps most telling is the willingness of supporters to engage in **personal sacrifice**. The January 6th Capitol riot demonstrated how deeply some followers were committed to Trump's cause. Many faced prison sentences yet continued to express loyalty, seeing themselves as martyrs rather than criminals.

By recognizing these cult-like dynamics, we gain insight into why Trumpism remains impervious to traditional political accountability. It is not just a policy platform—it is an identity-centered belief system, reinforced by fear, loyalty, and emotional bonding.

The Role of Fear and Grievance Politics in Solidifying Group Identity

Fear is one of the most potent tools in politics. In the Trump era, fear has been weaponized to keep supporters engaged and emotionally dependent on the leader. Issues like immigration, crime, socialism, and election integrity are framed as urgent threats, creating a state of perpetual alarm that reinforces loyalty[9].

Scapegoating is central to this strategy. Trump has blamed immigrants, minorities, journalists, and political elites for America's economic and cultural problems, deflecting attention from more complex causes. Instead of grappling with globalization or automation, his rhetoric points to familiar targets: "They're taking your jobs," or "They want to destroy the country."

Grievance politics is equally powerful. Trump positions himself as the defender of "forgotten Americans"—those who feel overlooked by coastal elites, government institutions, or cultural shifts. By validating these grievances and offering convenient scapegoats, he forges a connection so emotional that facts and policies take a back seat.

At the heart of this dynamic is the notion of **victimhood**. Trump and his base frequently portray themselves as persecuted by the media, Democrats, and the "Deep State." This fosters a shared identity built around resistance and resentment. Criticizing Trump often feels, to his supporters, like a personal attack—which only deepens their loyalty.

Another mechanism is **moral panic**—the belief that traditional values are under assault. Trump taps into fears about shifting cultural norms—from gender roles to religious expression—claiming that "woke ideology" is destroying the country. This framing unites supporters around a nostalgic vision of America and casts Trump as its final protector.

These fear-based tactics are powerful because they operate at an emotional level. As political theorist George Lakoff observed in *The Political Mind*[5], "Emotion is not the enemy of reason. It is essential to reason. Emotion makes reason possible. But strong emotions—like fear—can also override rationality when tribal identity is at stake."

When people feel threatened—psychologically, culturally, or economically—they are less receptive to new information. Research shows that fear can override rational thought, making it harder for fact-checking or debate to change minds[10].

Case Studies: GOP Politicians Punished for Speaking Out

One of the clearest signs of a cult-like political movement is the **punishment of dissenters**. As journalist McKay Coppins wrote in *The Atlantic*[11], "The party of ideas has become the party of loyalty. To oppose Trump, even on principle, is to risk political exile." In recent years, prominent Republicans who criticized Trump have—despite their conservative records—been marginalized or pushed out of the party.

Liz Cheney, the daughter of former Vice President Dick Cheney, had a strong conservative résumé: tax cuts, military expansion, and foreign policy hawkishness. Yet her vocal condemnation of Trump's role in the January 6th insurrection, and her participation in the congressional investigation, led to her ousting. In 2022, she lost her seat in the Wyoming primary to a Trump-endorsed challenger, despite previously enjoying overwhelming support.

Adam Kinzinger, a military veteran and long-serving Republican from Illinois, faced similar backlash after supporting Trump's second impeachment and denouncing election fraud claims. Rather than face certain defeat in a hostile party climate, he chose not to seek reelection in 2022.

Other examples abound. Jeff Flake and Bob Corker, both sitting Senators, opted not to run for reelection after criticizing Trump. Mitt Romney, the only Republican to vote for Trump's conviction in both impeachment trials, was censured by his state party and vilified by the conservative media ecosystem.

This trend reveals a fundamental shift in the Republican Party: loyalty to Trump now outweighs principle or policy[12]. Those who dissent are labeled as traitors, not fellow conservatives with different views. Internal debate is replaced by orthodoxy, enforced through primary challenges, public shaming, or outright expulsion.

Such **suppression of dissent** mirrors tactics used in authoritarian regimes. Rather than debate ideas, political figures are removed or discredited for failing to show loyalty to the leader. The GOP's transformation from an ideologically diverse coalition to a monolithic pro-Trump bloc has weakened democratic norms and made accountability more difficult.

Conclusion: Confronting Tribalism to Preserve Democracy

A functioning democracy requires dissent, debate, and internal accountability. When loyalty to a single leader overshadows these norms, parties risk sliding into authoritarianism[9]. The rise of blind tribalism, especially when it takes on cult-like behavior, poses a serious threat to democratic society.

When leaders are insulated from criticism and followers reject factual evidence, misinformation spreads unchecked, dissenters are silenced, and institutions are eroded. Restoring balance requires more than policy solutions—it requires cultural and psychological resilience.

We must create environments that promote critical thinking, welcome disagreement, and encourage people to examine their beliefs without fear of social or emotional cost. Media reform, civic education, and emotionally intelligent dialogue are essential tools in this effort.

Yet even as some voters fall into cult-like loyalty, others support the same party for very different reasons. Not all Republican voters are misled by lies. Many Republican voters support the party for reasons beyond misinformation, and are driven by self-interest, tradition, or disaffection—not delusion. In Part Two, we explore the diverse motivations behind GOP support, and how political identity, history, and grievance shape loyalty—even among those who see through the misinformation.

Part Two: Understanding the Appeal—
Why So Many Are Vulnerable

Part One explored the roots of false belief—how lies take hold through bias, manipulation, and media distortion. Part Two turns to a deeper question: *Why do so many people support a movement built on those beliefs, even if they don't fully believe them?*

Many Americans support Donald Trump because his message resonates with long-standing frustrations and deep distrust of national institutions.

The chapters that follow examine the roots of **political susceptibility**—not just the methods by which ignorance is seeded, but the conditions in which it takes hold.

For decades, conservative identity has been shaped in opposition to what many on the right perceive as an out-of-touch elite: from bureaucrats and media elites to scientists and celebrities. Trump didn't create that opposition—but he turned it into a powerful political weapon.

Part Two begins by distinguishing between different types of Trump supporters, recognizing that not all are conspiracy theorists or media zealots. Some are pragmatists. Others are loyalists, cultural traditionalists, or deeply religious conservatives who see their values threatened by rapid social change. Understanding this diversity is essential—not because every viewpoint is fact-based or morally defensible, but because meaningful discourse depends on recognizing what motivates people. To challenge misinformation effectively, we must first understand the emotional, cultural, and ideological forces that make certain narratives appealing—even to those who may not fully believe them.

Subsequent chapters explore how conservative mistrust of government and media has evolved, gradually eroding the shared information landscape and enabling alternate realities to flourish. We also examine how moral psychology and religious identity reinforce rigid worldviews, offering reassurance and moral certainty—but also closing people off to new ideas.

Part Two acknowledges that not all Republican voters are victims of disinformation. But even those who are not directly deceived often participate in—or help sustain—a system that spreads confusion, rewards loyalty over truth, and treats critical thinking as disloyalty.

Together, these chapters provide a deeper understanding of the emotional, cultural, and historical forces that shape modern conservative thought—and explain why, even when confronted with clear facts, many Americans remain unmoved.

Chapter 6

Not All Believers: Understanding the Republican Voter Base

Not everyone who supports Donald Trump—or the modern Republican Party—has been deceived by disinformation. Some voters don't fully believe the lies. Others don't care whether they're true.

For millions of Americans, Republican loyalty is shaped less by ideology than by habit, social identity, or economic interest. Some vote Republican because their families always have. Others vote Republican because it benefits them financially—or because politics has become more about loyalty than truth: as long as their team is winning, truth is negotiable.

Misinformation may still be present in these cases, but it's not the driving force. These voters are motivated by stability, familiarity, or resentment, not necessarily false belief. Their choices are shaped more by incentives and social cues than ideological conviction.

And in many cases, the choice is less about enthusiasm for the party's message than discomfort with the alternative. Some vote out of resignation. Others vote out of fear—of social and economic change, or perceived threats to their way of life.

These nuances are often overlooked in political analysis. But they matter. They help explain how support can persist even among those who see through the deception—and why disinformation doesn't need to be universally believed to be politically effective.

Recognizing this distinction helps us move beyond the notion that all Republican voters are irrational or misinformed—and opens the door to a deeper understanding of why support persists even among those who know better.

The Voter Is Not Always the Believer

Ignorance today is not just passive—it's cultivated and exploited. But not all affected by disinformation are convinced by it. Some knowingly vote for dishonest politicians. Others repeat talking points they suspect are false. Many avoid political information entirely, relying on heuristics—party label, tradition, or instinct—to guide choices.

Support for a political party does not require belief in every claim it makes. Just as Democrats may vote blue while disagreeing with certain policies, Republican voters can support Trump or the GOP without internalizing every narrative. For some, voting is less about facts than about identity.

Polls show[1] that many Republicans believe falsehoods—like the 2020 election being stolen. But belief exists on a spectrum. Some genuinely accept conspiracy theories. Others signal loyalty. Others simply echo what they've heard, without reflection.

If we assume all Republican voters are deluded, we risk misreading their motivations—and alienating those who might otherwise be open to reason. It's entirely possible to support a dishonest candidate while acknowledging their dishonesty: "All politicians lie. At least he's on my side." In such cases, the lie gets excused—not embraced.

This connects to motivated reasoning, but with a twist: instead of changing beliefs to match propaganda, some voters just dismiss its relevance. Political scientist Jason Brennan describes this as **rational ignorance**—the idea that it's not worth sorting through complex or conflicting information when daily life is shaped more by local realities than political abstractions. As Brennan puts it[2], "Most voters are ignorant not because they're stupid but because it's rational for them to be ignorant"—a pragmatic choice in a system where information rarely changes outcomes.

Disinformation still shapes the broader narrative—but not always individual belief. For many, political lies are background noise—a familiar hum they've learned to ignore.

This helps explain why fact-checking often fails. When lies are tolerated rather than believed, correcting them misses the point. As media critic Brian Stelter wrote[3], "If everything is spin, then nothing matters. And if nothing matters, the lie wins"—a succinct diagnosis of the disinformation era. The issue isn't always whether something's false—but whether it matters. For some Republican voters, it doesn't.

Understanding this mindset isn't excusing it. Indifference to truth still enables manipulation and undermines democracy. But if we want to bridge divides—or at least understand them—we must distinguish between those who are misled and those who are unconcerned.

The Transactional Voter—Bottom Line Above All

Many Republican voters support Trump not because of ideology or identity—but because of their **bottom line**. These are **transactional voters**, who approach politics as a cost-benefit calculation.

This isn't new. Voters have always asked, "What's in it for me?" For some, the answer is lower taxes. For others, deregulation, pro-business policies, or a bullish stock market. These voters may dislike Trump's behavior or rhetoric—but tolerate it if they believe they're financially better off.

This logic is **pragmatic**. Many small business owners, professionals, and upper-income voters see themselves as beneficiaries of Republican policy. They aren't watching cable news obsessively. They suspect Trump lies—but **compartmentalize**. If the financial gains outweigh the moral costs, they accept the trade.

A 2020 Pew study[4] found economic concerns— especially tax and regulation policy—were top reasons Trump voters cited for their support, even among those with doubts about his character.

For these voters, political lies are like side effects on a prescription label: unpleasant but tolerable if the medication works. Some acknowledge the dangers—and justify them: "Yes, he's dishonest, but he gets results."

This logic also applies to broader interests—corporate growth, inheritance protection, or preserving economic hierarchies. For many white-collar or affluent suburban voters, the GOP represents stability, or at least the appearance of it.

Transactional politics isn't inherently unethical. But when material benefit becomes the only concern, it creates space for authoritarianism. A leader who promises prosperity can violate norms, lie, or erode institutions—if the payoff seems worth it.

Disinformation becomes toxic here not by converting people into believers—but by **numbing them into tolerance**. These voters may not spread lies—but they normalize the liars.

They often see themselves as realists—too smart for spin, too focused for distraction. But when truth is sacrificed for profit, the end result is the same: a system where lies flourish, accountability fades, and democracy decays.

The Traditionalist—Voting by Heritage, Not Argument

For another segment of the base, voting isn't about ideology or economics. It's about **continuity**. These are the **traditionalist voters**—people who support the GOP because that's what their family or community has always done.

In many populations—especially rural towns, religious communities, and older generations—Republican identity is part of everyday life. The GOP isn't just a party—it's a symbol of belonging. Voting Republican becomes an expression of loyalty to family, faith, or community. As Ezra Klein notes[5], "Most people inherit their political views like heirlooms. They don't examine them. They just carry them"—a pattern especially visible in traditionalist voting behavior.

This isn't unique to conservatives. But for many older Republican voters, the label signifies **patriotism, morality, and order**—even if the party's policies or leaders have changed. In such settings, party affiliation is less about policy and more about cultural identity.

Media habits reinforce this. If Fox News or conservative talk radio has been part of someone's daily routine for decades, it becomes a trusted voice. When a familiar source says something, it feels true—less because of logic than because of familiarity.

This isn't willful ignorance—it's about **not questioning what feels natural**. Admitting that trusted media outlets are peddling propaganda isn't just uncomfortable—it feels like betrayal.

This makes traditionalist voters hard to persuade. They aren't angry ideologues or greedy cynics. They're people whose identity is tied to their vote. Challenging their political alignment can feel like attacking their heritage.

Psychologically, this reflects **identity-protective cognition**[6]—our tendency to reject information that threatens group identity. When politics is about belonging, facts take a back seat to emotional coherence.

Traditionalists may repeat misinformation in polls, but often not because they've deeply considered it. They repeat what aligns with their world. The disinformation reflects **social alignment**, not belief.

The challenge is profound. Traditionalist voters are often decent, civic-minded people—but their trust has been captured by institutions that have abused it. The result isn't just misinformation—it's misplaced confidence.

Persuading them may require shared values and personal trust—not more fact-checking. These voters aren't unreachable. But any path forward begins by recognizing that familiarity, not logic, often guides belief.

The Disengaged Voter—Apathy, Alienation, Noise

Not all Republican voters are ideologically committed or culturally anchored. Some are simply checked out. These are the **disengaged voters**—individuals who participate in elections out of habit, duty, or vague preference, but who avoid political information, ignore policy debates, and often express frustration or fatigue with the political system as a whole.

For this group, **politics feels like noise**—confusing, overwhelming, or irrelevant to their daily lives. They may still cast a vote for Republican candidates, but their decision is often based on a vague sense of party identity or personal instinct rather than careful consideration. They are not watching Fox News every night. They are not analyzing legislative platforms. They are not poring over fact-checks or opinion columns. They are busy, distracted, and often skeptical that any politician—Left or Right—has their best interests in mind.

This kind of disengagement is more widespread than many realize. Studies have consistently shown that a significant portion of the American electorate is **politically inattentive**. A 2022 Pew Research Center study[7] found that only about one-third of U.S. adults say they follow government and politics "most of the time." The rest either follow only occasionally or not at all. Among these low-engagement voters, party loyalty is often inherited, reinforced by social surroundings, or based on broad impressions rather than specific beliefs.

Disengaged voters may describe themselves as "independent" or "moderate," but their actual voting behavior often aligns with one party—usually the one they've associated with for most of their lives. In conservative regions, that default is typically Republican. These voters are not necessarily hostile to Democrats, but they aren't interested in parsing policy differences or investigating political claims. They **vote for the familiar**, often based on surface impressions: who seems strong, who sounds confident, who looks like a leader.

Disinformation can affect this group in subtle but powerful ways. Even if they don't fully believe the false claims circulating in the media, they're often exposed to them repeatedly, through social media, casual conversations, or passive news consumption. Over time, these messages create **ambient distrust**. They may not believe that the 2020 election was stolen, but they've heard "there were some problems." And even if they don't buy into conspiracies, they've absorbed the idea that "the media can't be trusted."

This creates a hazy informational environment where no one seems reliable—a condition that benefits those who are most willing to manipulate truth. When facts are hard to distinguish from spin, and when everyone seems biased, many voters retreat into cynicism and detachment. The result is not just misinformation, but political nihilism: a sense that nothing really matters, and that all sides are equally bad.

From a psychological standpoint, this disengagement is a form of **cognitive conservation**[8]. Faced with complex and conflicting information, people often default to mental shortcuts—party labels, candidate image, or community consensus. These shortcuts reduce cognitive effort, but they also leave voters vulnerable to manipulation. When the truth is hard to verify and trust is low, people often rely on instinct over evidence.

Disengaged voters are not unreachable, but they are difficult to engage. Appeals to truth, policy, or morality may fall flat if those concepts feel abstract or irrelevant. What resonates more often are personal stories, local concerns, and relationships built over time. These voters don't need lectures. They need reasons to care.

In some ways, the disengaged voter represents a greater long-term challenge than the true believer. They do not defend disinformation—but they do fail to resist it. Apathy becomes complicity. Detachment clears the way for deception. And cynicism gives cover to those who lie. And their indifference allows misinformation to spread unchecked. Anti-apartheid activist Steve Biko once warned[9], "The most potent weapon in the hands of the oppressor is the mind of the oppressed"—a reminder that disengagement, even if passive, serves the interests of those in power.

A healthy democracy depends not only on free and fair elections, but on an electorate that is **informed, engaged, and invested**. When large swaths of voters turn away from the political process—either out of exhaustion or resignation—the door opens for those who are willing to exploit that vacuum. The disengaged may not be the loudest voices in our politics, but their silence creates space for the worst actors to take the stage. As the philosopher Plato allegedly warned, "The price good men pay for indifference to public affairs is to be ruled by evil men."

The Tribal Realist—Truth Is Secondary to Winning

Some Republican voters know the lies—and support them anyway. These are the **tribal realists**: people who view politics as a zero-sum competition between teams. And they intend to win.

Tribal realists follow news, debate issues, and recognize propaganda. But they use information as a weapon, not a lens. They may doubt conspiracy theories, but pivot to bigger grievances—liberal overreach, cancel culture, or political correctness. Their engagement is about **alignment**, not accuracy.

This mindset reflects decades of polarization and a media system that rewards outrage. Tribal realists know some claims are false—but embrace them publicly if they help the team. Politics is war. And in war, truth is a casualty. As Jonathan Haidt warns, "When loyalty to the tribe becomes more important than loyalty to the truth, truth loses."

This isn't traditional hypocrisy. It's **instrumental reasoning**: if lies defeat a dangerous opponent, so be it. The ends justify the means.

Years of partisan rhetoric—"they want to destroy America," "they hate freedom"—have framed politics as existential. In that frame, disinformation becomes a weapon, and rejecting it is seen as weakness.

As political scientist Lilliana Mason writes[10], "Partisanship is not just about policy—it's about who we are," underscoring how deeply political alignment can intertwine with personal identity. Social identity theory explains this. When political loyalty merges with cultural identity, dissent feels like betrayal. Tribal realists may reject specific lies, but still support the system that spreads them—because defeating the other side matters more than truth.

This group poses a distinct challenge because they possess critical thinking skills—but deploy them selectively. They may say, "He lies—but the other side is worse." It's not about the message. It's about the messenger.

This corrodes democracy. When truth is optional, manipulation becomes strategy. And lying becomes normalized.

The irony? Many tribal realists believe they're defending America's core values—freedom, patriotism, the Constitution. But in practice, they enable tactics that undermine those ideals.

Engaging them requires more than facts. It requires reframing the conversation around shared norms and long-term consequences. They aren't uninformed. They're deeply invested—in outcomes, not process. Until that changes, truth will remain a secondary concern.

The Danger of Indifference

While Republican voters differ in motivation—true believers, pragmatists, traditionalists, disengaged, tribal realists—many share a **tolerance for deception**. That tolerance, even when rationalized, has real consequences. It fosters a world where lies aren't just accepted—they're expected. Holocaust survivor Elie Wiesel put it simply[11]: "The opposite of love is not hate, it's indifference"—a haunting reminder of how disengagement enables injustice.

This indifference normalizes disinformation. When voters reward liars because they like the policies, identify with the party, or just don't care—it signals that **truth is optional**. And when truth is optional, accountability disappears.

Disinformation then becomes "just politics." Fact-checking is dismissed. Lies are shrugged off.

Democracy requires more than voting—it requires a **shared commitment to reality**.

This indifference empowers the worst actors. Trump thrives in a world where truth is flexible—and loyalty is firm. He exploits apathy, manipulates tribal loyalty, and counts on supporters not caring about accuracy.

Even voters who reject the lies still tolerate the liars. That gives cover to extremists. Silence becomes permission. As cult expert Steven Hassan observes[12], "In cultic environments, scandals don't destroy loyalty—they reinforce it," making the leader appear embattled and the loyalty seem righteous by contrast.

History shows that authoritarianism often rises not through mass deception—but through **mass inaction**[13]. The signs are visible. The lies are obvious. But comfort, cynicism, or loyalty overpower the will to resist.

Not all Republican voters are misinformed. Not all support Trump. But millions support a party that has embraced disinformation. Whether that support is driven by belief, habit, or interest—the effect is the same: a political culture unmoored from truth.

Why This Distinction Matters

Recognizing that not all Republican voters believe—or care about—the lies is not about sympathy. It's about clarity. Trump supporters are too often described as deluded or cult-like. That applies to some. But not to all.

Distinguishing among motivations allows for more effective strategy. Talking to a tribal realist is different from reaching a traditionalist. Engaging the disengaged means overcoming apathy, not correcting facts.

If the problem were just belief in lies, education might suffice. But when people accept lies as part of politics, or tune out completely, the issue is cultural, not just cognitive. Apathy and tribalism damage democracy as much as gullibility.

This distinction keeps our focus where it belongs: on a political movement that uses disinformation strategically. That strategy succeeds not only by convincing—but by **numbing, dividing, and distracting**. A disengaged or indifferent public is easy to manipulate.

Even when Republican voters aren't misinformed, their continued support **legitimizes a system built on falsehoods**. That's the deeper danger. Disinformation doesn't just mislead—it changes the rules, making lies a winning tactic and honesty a risk.

The next chapter explores those who *do* believe the lies. But to understand why disinformation succeeds, we must look beyond the content of the lies and examine the *environment* in which they spread—an environment shaped by decades of institutional distrust, political alienation, and cultural resentment. A movement built on falsehoods survives not only on belief—but also on habit, self-interest, and disconnection. And those are even harder to confront.

Chapter 7

Seeds of Distrust: Historical Grievances

For decades, surveys have tracked a steady erosion of public trust in America's core institutions. Gallup surveys show a long-term decline in public trust across nearly every major institution in American life[1]. Government, media, academia, and science—once seen as pillars of public life—have become, for many on the political right, symbols of corruption, elitism, or betrayal.

This growing distrust didn't begin with Trump, but it created fertile ground for his rise. The political climate that gave rise to Trumpism was already primed by years of frustration and alienation— fueled by cultural shifts, economic upheaval, and a sense of moral decline. Trump didn't invent this rift—he exploited it.

To understand how disinformation takes hold, we must first grasp the disillusionment that made so many Americans ready to believe it.

Betrayals and Backlashes

The 1960s and 1970s shattered the illusion that American institutions could be trusted to act in the public interest. Vietnam revealed not just military misjudgment, but systematic deception by government leaders. Watergate confirmed that political elites could engage in criminal conspiracies—and lie about them for years. For many conservatives, these events affirmed a deeply felt betrayal: that those who claimed moral or intellectual authority could not be believed.

At the same time, sweeping cultural shifts—civil rights legislation, feminist movements, and the sexual revolution—were embraced by elites in academia, the media, and coastal urban centers. But these changes often met resistance in more traditional communities that felt bypassed, judged, or dismissed. Barack Obama, during a 2008 fundraiser, touched off conservative outrage when he described[2] how some Americans in struggling communities "cling to guns or religion or antipathy to people who aren't like them" as a response to economic and cultural dislocation. Though intended as a sociological observation, many on the right took it as confirmation that elites looked down on them.

The 1973 Supreme Court decision in Roe v. Wade legalized abortion. Schools were integrated under federal mandate. Religious prayer disappeared from classrooms. These were not just policy shifts—to some, they felt like rejections of cherished values. While progressives celebrated these milestones, many conservatives experienced them as evidence that the country was moving forward without them—and in their eyes, against them.

Economic changes compounded disillusionment. The 1990s brought NAFTA, deindustrialization, and the offshoring of manufacturing jobs. Towns that had once thrived on steel, coal, or factory labor began to wither. For many working-class Americans, globalization was not an abstract policy—it was a devastating reality. As factories shut down and economic security vanished, the elite consensus around trade and open markets seemed indifferent to their pain. Meanwhile, politicians promised solutions but delivered little, reinforcing the idea that Washington was more interested in Wall Street than Main Street.

The Conservative Turn

In response, the American Right began to frame itself explicitly in opposition to these institutions. Ronald Reagan captured this conservative mood in 1986 with a line that would become legend[3]: "The nine most terrifying words in the English language are: 'I'm from the government, and I'm here to help.'" This sentiment framed government as inherently suspect—an attitude that still shapes Right-wing politics today. Government was no longer the solution. It was the problem.

The 1980s also saw the rise of conservative talk radio, led by figures like Rush Limbaugh, who built massive audiences by ridiculing liberal elites, mocking political correctness, and portraying conservatives as the victims of an out-of-touch establishment.

Limbaugh, whose voice defined conservative talk radio for decades, once described America[4] as divided between "the old-fashioned, God-fearing, patriotic, taxpaying, law-abiding, hard-working America" and "the liberal America—the America of the elites." Limbaugh's message turned grievance into identity. His depiction of two Americas—one hard-working and moral, the other elite and out of touch—shaped the tone of conservative media for decades. His style was confrontational, often inflammatory, and rooted in the idea that traditional Americans were under siege from coastal, secular, academic elites.

The term "silent majority," coined by Nixon[5] and embraced by Reagan[6,7], offered conservatives a new identity: not just voters, but cultural guardians. They were no longer just arguing policy—they were defending a way of life. This blend of grievance and righteousness created a powerful sense of purpose: to protect the nation from those who would reshape it in the image of San Francisco, Harvard, or The New York Times.

Race also played a significant—if often unspoken—role in this shift. Policies like desegregation and affirmative action became flashpoints for conservatives. They were seen as signs that the government was favoring others at their expense. Reagan's infamous invocation[8] of the "welfare queen" was no accident—it spoke to a deeper cultural resentment that government had turned its back on working-class whites while catering to minorities, immigrants, and outsiders.

Anti-Elitism and the Rise of Populist Framing

Over time, this skepticism evolved into full-blown anti-elitism. To many on the Right, the media weren't merely biased—they were actively working against conservative values. Universities were no longer centers of learning, but corrupting young minds with leftist indoctrination. Newt Gingrich, architect of the 1994 "Contract with America," helped deepen conservative suspicion of universities and media, warning[9] that "the academic, the news media, and the secular bureaucratic system ... all hate our values." For many on the Right, it wasn't just that these institutions were liberal—it was that they were hostile. Hollywood wasn't just out of touch—it was a moral cesspool. For many conservatives, this wasn't mere paranoia—it was a worldview shaped by decades of perceived betrayal.

Evangelical churches and conservative media offered refuge. Christian radio, megachurches, and family-friendly networks created alternative communities where mainstream narratives were dismissed and biblical or traditionalist perspectives prevailed. These spaces didn't just offer news or theology—they offered a place to belong.

As the internet matured, this alternative ecosystem grew stronger. Websites, forums, and eventually social media made it easier to find like-minded voices and reject mainstream authority. The idea that "experts" looked down on ordinary Americans wasn't just a talking point—it felt true. Fact-checkers, scientists, and journalists were increasingly seen as part of an insular class with no respect for conservative values or lived experience. Trump's former strategist Steve Bannon reportedly summed up his media strategy[10] as "flood the zone with shit"—a blunt acknowledgment that overwhelming the public with disinformation isn't a failure of the system—it's a deliberate tactic of authoritarian messaging.

By the 2000s, a populist narrative had taken hold: America was being run by a coastal, globalist elite that mocked real Americans, outsourced their jobs, and rewrote their history. This story—of loss, exclusion, and righteous anger—was waiting for a champion.

Enter Trump

Donald Trump didn't invent these grievances. He inherited them—and then amplified them with ruthless precision. Where other politicians spoke in code, Trump spoke plainly. Trump didn't merely acknowledge conservative resentment—he amplified it. "They're not after me," he told supporters. "They're after you. I'm just in the way."

Trump's appeal was as visceral as it was political. He channeled decades of conservative frustration into a single persona: brash, combative, unapologetic. He attacked the media, mocked the experts, and insulted the elite—all while claiming to speak for the forgotten American.

In 2017, Donald Trump tweeted[11]: "The fake news media … is not my enemy, it is the enemy of the American people." To his supporters, this wasn't hyperbole—it was confirmation. If the media were aligned against Trump, it must be aligned against them too. For those who had spent decades feeling ignored or belittled, Trump was a vindication. He was proof that someone—finally—was willing to fight dirty on their behalf.

The more the media criticized him, the more his supporters saw it as validation. The more experts warned against him, the more people tuned them out. In Trump's world, institutions couldn't be trusted—but he could. After all, he was hated by all the right people.

How Grievance Became Vulnerability

Grievance alone doesn't cause disinformation to flourish. But it creates fertile ground for it to take root. When people feel unheard, devalued, or erased, they are more likely to embrace explanations that confirm their suffering—and to reject sources that challenge their worldview.

For millions of Americans, belief in conspiracy theories wasn't about gullibility—it was about trust. They didn't trust the media to tell them the truth. They didn't trust scientists to admit mistakes. They didn't trust politicians to act in good faith. In this context, claims about George Soros funding migrant caravans, or a "Deep State" plotting against the president, didn't seem absurd. They seemed plausible. Even logical.

Grievance primes the mind for tribalism. If the system is rigged, then only loyalty matters. If institutions are compromised, then anyone who challenges your side must be part of the enemy. This is why claims of voter fraud and stolen elections spread—not because the evidence supported them, but because the emotional groundwork had already been laid.

Conclusion: From Alienation to Alignment

The rise of Trumpism cannot be understood without acknowledging the long history of distrust and disillusionment that paved its way. Conservative frustration wasn't irrational. Many had, in fact, been left behind or dismissed. That pain is real. But when that pain is exploited—when legitimate grievances are funneled into conspiracy, fear, and blind loyalty—it becomes a danger not only to those who believe it, but to the democracy they inhabit.

Understanding this evolution doesn't excuse the outcomes. But it reveals why even intelligent, informed people can fall into patterns of belief that seem bewildering to outsiders. It wasn't a single event, a single lie, or a single man that created this political reality. It was years—decades— of alienation and cultural displacement.

And once you stop trusting anyone, you're vulnerable to trusting the wrong one. James Baldwin warned[12] that "people who shut their eyes to reality simply invite their own destruction." When institutions are distrusted by default, and conspiracy becomes common sense, the collapse of democratic norms is no longer hypothetical—it's inevitable.

But the void left by institutional distrust isn't always filled with chaos. For many, it's a **clear moral worldview**—rooted in faith, tradition, or identity.

In the next chapter, we explore how the political right offers not just information or ideology, but a moral framework that helps millions of people feel grounded in a culture they believe is slipping away.

Chapter 8

Faith, Fear, and Fox: The Moral Framework of Conservative America

For many conservatives, politics isn't just a matter of policy—it's often an expression of values and identity—deeply rooted in moral conviction. That's why traditional liberal appeals to logic, evidence, or fact-checking often fall flat—they don't speak the same moral language. To understand the enduring appeal of Trump—and the worldview that sustains it—we must examine the moral architecture of conservative America.

This chapter explores that framework: how religious faith, moral psychology, and partisan media ecosystems combine to offer a sense of moral order in an increasingly unstable culture. It's not just about partisanship—it's about purpose. For millions of Americans, the political right offers not just a team to cheer for, but a moral compass in a culture they no longer recognize.

Why Left and Right See the World Differently

Psychologist Jonathan Haidt, whose work on **moral foundations theory** reshaped political psychology, explains[1] that "liberals and conservatives rely on different sets of moral foundations… which is why they often talk past one another." Liberals tend to prioritize *care* and *fairness,* especially when it comes to equity and harm reduction. Conservatives, by contrast, are more attuned to *loyalty*, *authority*, and *sanctity*. They reflect a preference for preserving social order and honoring traditional structures of authority.

This doesn't mean conservatives lack empathy, or that liberals have no respect for rules. It means their instinctive reactions to political issues are grounded in **different intuitive triggers**. To a liberal, separating immigrant families is a moral outrage. To a conservative, it may be seen as a necessary act to uphold order and sovereignty.

These distinct moral "taste buds," as Haidt calls them, help explain why the same protest, court ruling, or scientific recommendation can be interpreted in radically different ways, depending on one's worldview. And when these frameworks are paired with tribal identity, they become more rigid, more emotionally charged, and more resistant to challenge. Cognitive linguist George Lakoff has argued[2] that "conservatives have mastered moral framing. They don't just argue policies—they tell moral stories." Such stories resonate deeply, shaping how people interpret events and justify decisions.

Religious Identity and Moral Certainty

One of the most influential sources of moral identity for American conservatives is evangelical Christianity. For decades, it has offered not only theological guidance but also a cultural worldview. It includes belief in absolute truth, a cosmic struggle between good and evil, and a clear divide between righteousness and corruption.

Within that framework, social changes—on issues like LGBTQ rights, gender roles, or secular education—are not simply disagreements. They are threats to a divinely ordered society. As sociologist Robert P. Jones observes[3], "White Christian nationalism is not just a political ideology—it's a cultural identity that sacralizes the myth of a 'Christian America.'" For many conservative evangelicals, political battles feel like religious ones.

The idea that America was founded as a Christian nation is central to this identity. As mainstream culture becomes more diverse and secular, many conservative Christians experience this as a kind of **cultural exile**—a sense that they are being pushed out of the country their ancestors built.

Though lacking personal piety, Trump offered Evangelicals something few other politicians did: unconditional affirmation. He didn't ask for their approval—he demanded it—and in doing so, he made them feel powerful again. Historian Kristin Kobes Du Mez writes[4] that for many evangelicals, "Donald Trump functioned as a protector—a strongman who would defend Christianity and restore America's moral order." His brashness wasn't a liability—it was an asset.

This religious loyalty is further reinforced by media figures and pastors who frame political battles in biblical terms. Elections are framed not as contests, but as spiritual tests—where opponents are cast not as wrong, but as wicked. In this view, facts are less important than allegiance. When morality is cast in absolute terms, compromise becomes betrayal, and nuance becomes weakness.

Fear, Order, and the Conservative Brain

Neuroscientific and psychological research has shown that individuals who identify as conservative are, on average, more sensitive to threats. Political scientist John Hibbing notes[5] that conservatives tend to be more "threat-sensitive," meaning they are more likely to respond strongly to images or messages related to disorder or danger—even when the threats are exaggerated. This doesn't mean they are paranoid—it means they are attuned to danger, disorder, and change. What once served as an evolutionary advantage now makes fear-based messaging especially potent.

Conservatives often prefer stability over experimentation, and hierarchy over ambiguity. They tend to see the world as a place where **clear rules and strong authority** are necessary to maintain order. As a result, policies or cultural shifts that introduce uncertainty—immigration surges, gender nonconformity, rapidly changing norms—are experienced as existential disruptions.

Trump's messaging—focused on crime, invasion, chaos, and national decline—spoke directly to these instincts. He didn't offer complexity; he offered control. And for many people overwhelmed by social change and economic insecurity, that simplicity felt like safety. Journalist Amanda Ripley writes[6], "When people feel threatened, they tend to become more tribal—and less curious." Fear narrows thinking. It turns moral questions into battles for survival.

This orientation also helps explain the appeal of authoritarian leadership styles. Authoritarian figures who speak in absolutes, attack opponents, and reject compromise may repel liberals—but to those primed to value authority and order, they can be reassuring.

Media as Moral Authority

Conservative media has long understood its role is not just to report news, but to interpret events through a moral lens. From Rush Limbaugh to Sean Hannity to religious broadcasters, the goal has never been simple neutrality—it's moral clarity. Right and wrong. Patriots and traitors. Us versus them.

Fox News, in particular, perfected this formula. Its segments are not designed to inform—they are designed to affirm. To give viewers a sense of outrage, righteousness, and belonging. The same is true of Right-wing influencers on YouTube, podcasts, and social media: they craft narratives that reinforce identity and sustain the belief that their audience is **under siege by immoral forces**.

Tucker Carlson once warned his audience[7], "They're trying to destroy everything you love about this country," tapping into the deep-seated conservative belief that mainstream America is under siege—not politically, but morally.

The repetition of moral panic themes—"they're grooming your children," "they want to take your guns," "they hate Christianity"—fosters an emotional dependency. Viewers come to expect outrage, and to need it. Each scandal becomes another chapter in the long war between the righteous and the wicked.

Over time, partisan media consumption can become a form of tribal worship. The facts may be distorted or even fabricated—but they *feel* true. And in moral reasoning, feeling often overrides evidence. Media theorist Neil Postman warned[8], "Americans are the best entertained and least informed people in the world." For many conservative viewers, partisan media isn't just affirming—it's addictive, offering drama, emotion, and moral affirmation in place of civic engagement.

Outrage as Identity

In a fragmented and alienating world, outrage becomes a source of emotional cohesion. Shared anger unites people. It gives them purpose. It defines the in-group, and exposes the out-group. Trump instinctively harnessed this dynamic. His rallies were not policy seminars—they were rituals of shared grievance, where supporters chant slogans and cheer their defiance.

This intensity makes cross-political engagement increasingly difficult. When identity is fused with outrage, disagreement becomes impossible. Any challenge to Trump, or to conservative orthodoxy, is interpreted not as a difference of opinion—but as a personal attack, a betrayal, or even a form of spiritual warfare.

Social media amplifies this even further. Algorithms tend to elevate the most inflammatory content, not because it's true—but because it's engaging. Memes, soundbites, and viral clips fuel the sense that the world is burning—and that only those who are truly "awake" can see it.

In this environment, facts are flexible, but feelings are fixed. If something makes people angry or afraid, they believe it must be true. Hannah Arendt cautioned[9] that totalitarian propaganda "relies on emotional coherence rather than factual accuracy." When people are guided by outrage and fear, they become easier to manipulate—and harder to persuade.

The Comfort of Righteous Certainty

What ties all of this together is a yearning for clarity in a world that feels increasingly unstable. Religious traditions and partisan storytelling offer something reality often cannot: certainty. You are good. They are evil. Your side is righteous. The other is corrupted.

This kind of black-and-white thinking is comforting. It relieves the burden of doubt and critical thinking. And in a time when traditional structures— church attendance, civic organizations, local media— are in decline, moral absolutism fills the void.

Trump offered that certainty. He never wavered, never apologized, never compromised. His followers didn't care about consistency—they admired conviction. He was imperfect—but to many, he was "fighting for us." In a culture where people felt morally abandoned, Trump became their moral avenger.

That's why debunking and fact-checking so often fail to resonate. It's not that the facts don't matter—it's that they don't *function* the same way. When politics is faith, doubt is heresy. And for many conservatives, Trump's role is not to inform, but to defend.

Conclusion: Understanding the Appeal, Confronting the Manipulation

This moral framework is not inherently toxic. Loyalty, tradition, order, and spiritual meaning are deeply human values. They bind communities, preserve history, and offer comfort in difficult times. But when those values are exploited—when faith becomes fanaticism or fear becomes fuel for division— they become dangerous.

Understanding this moral lens does not mean agreeing with it. But it helps explain why so many people seem impervious to facts, why Trump's appeal endures, and why traditional political discourse so often fails. To reach across divides—or even to understand them—we must see that people aren't just choosing policies. They're choosing moral worlds.

And in a world that feels morally chaotic, the loudest voice promising clarity will always have a captive audience. Psychiatrist Bandy X. Lee notes[10] that "when people feel insecure or threatened, they will gravitate toward authoritarian figures who project strength and certainty." This is especially true when institutions seem to waver or contradict themselves.

That's what makes Trump's rise so revealing—and so dangerous. His appeal wasn't built on policy or performance, but on the promise of clarity in a world that felt unstable. Part 3 examines how that promise became a political force—fueled by grievance and reinforced by hyper-partisan media.

Part Three: The Trump Phenomenon & Cult of Misinformation

Donald Trump's political rise was not an anomaly. It emerged from forces that had already begun reshaping American politics: a fragmented media ecosystem that splintered public discourse, deepening mistrust of institutions, and identity movements fueled by cultural resentment. He didn't just run a campaign—he built a movement that elevated loyalty over truth and turned defiance of expertise into a badge of honor.

Part Three explores why Trump's appeal has remained so resilient—despite a cascade of indictments and mounting evidence of misconduct. His success lies not just in charisma, but in his ability to amplify public disillusionment and cast himself in a role that defies contradiction—at once savior and victim.

These chapters examine how Trump reshaped public perception through repetition and narrative control, how the GOP aligned itself with his image, and how misinformation became a tool of governance.

By understanding these dynamics, we can begin to assess the deeper impact of Trumpism: the erosion of shared truth, the rise of authoritarian tactics, and the structural challenges that lie ahead. Confronting weaponized political ignorance is no longer just a matter of truth versus lies—it is a test of whether democratic norms can survive the storm.

Chapter 9

Why Do People Believe Trump?

Trump's appeal extends well beyond traditional political boundaries. His ability to retain a loyal base despite scandals and failures raises an urgent question: *What drives the intensity of this support?*

The answer lies in a powerful combination: authoritarian psychology, grievance politics, identity-based loyalty, and the strategic use of disinformation.

The Strong Leader Archetype and Authoritarian Psychology

One of the key reasons Trump retains unwavering support is the perception that he is a strong leader. Research in political psychology shows that people are often drawn to **authoritarian-style leadership**[1], especially in times of social and economic instability. These leaders project confidence, offer simple solutions, and claim to be the only ones capable of fixing a broken system. This appeal is strongest among those who feel powerless and prefer decisive action over drawn-out deliberation. As political scientists

Steven Levitsky and Daniel Ziblatt explain in *How Democracies Die*[2], "Authoritarians often rise by exploiting the disillusionment of ordinary people, presenting themselves as the only force capable of restoring order and control."

Trump has carefully cultivated this image. His slogans—"I alone can fix it," "drain the swamp," and "witch hunt"—cast him as a bold outsider fighting against entrenched corruption[3]. His combative style, personal attacks on opponents, and disregard for political norms are often viewed by supporters as signs of strength, not flaws.

This impression is further supported by **charismatic leadership**, which relies on emotional connection rather than rational policy appeal. Political theorist Yascha Mounk, in *The People vs. Democracy*[4], explains that "charismatic populists offer emotional reassurance rather than solutions; their appeal lies not in competence but in affective connection." Trump's unscripted, repetitive, and grievance-driven speeches resonate with those who feel alienated. His ability to provoke emotion and offer black-and-white solutions creates a psychological bond that traditional politicians rarely achieve.

Authoritarian-leaning individuals tend to prefer hierarchical structures and value strength over pluralism. Trump's refusal to admit error, his disregard for expertise, and his relentless attacks on institutions are often interpreted by his base as resolve, not wrongdoing[5]. In contrast to traditional leaders who apologize or adjust their positions, Trump often reinforces this image by doubling down instead of walking back controversial claims, reinforcing the image of someone who never yields—a trait many supporters admire.

This strongman persona was firmly established by his role on *The Apprentice*[6], where he was portrayed as a decisive, successful businessman. Millions watched him fire contestants and deliver grand pronouncements, reinforcing a public image that persists despite multiple bankruptcies and questionable business practices.

In truth, Trump's business record includes six bankruptcies—including a casino—and poor returns relative to the $400 million he inherited[7]. Yet many supporters appear unpersuaded by these facts, embracing Trump as an avatar of resilience and leadership—regardless of the facts.

His appeal stems less from policy or governance than from the emotional bond he builds with supporters and the image of unshakable dominance he projects. Sociologist Arlie Russell Hochschild, in *Strangers in Their Own Land*[8], found that "supporters didn't care whether Trump could deliver—they felt he spoke their anger and gave voice to their humiliation."

Trump has masterfully tapped into the grievances of disaffected Americans—especially among white working-class voters who feel economically and culturally left behind. By branding himself the champion of forgotten Americans, he offers more than policy: he delivers **emotional validation**[9]. This connection is built not only on economic promises but on a shared cultural narrative rooted in perceived loss and injustice.

Many Americans have faced job losses due to globalization, automation, and economic shifts. Rather than address these structural issues through policy, Trump simplifies the narrative. He often attributes these challenges to immigrants, foreign nations, or liberal elites, offering easy scapegoats for supporters to blame. This framing offers emotionally satisfying, though simplified, explanations for complex problems. In *American Carnage*[10], journalist Tim Alberta observes, "For Trump, grievance was not merely a campaign theme—it was a governing principle. The appeal of victimhood became a political identity."

Beyond economics, Trump taps into **cultural anxieties**. For many of his followers, increasing visibility of minority groups, LGBTQ+ rights, and progressive social movements represents a loss of traditional status. Trump's rhetoric—attacking "woke culture," dismissing diversity initiatives, and championing "real Americans"—validates those who feel displaced by these changes.

His slogan, "Make America Great Again," offers a nostalgic vision of a time when many of his supporters felt more secure and dominant. This **cultural displacement**—real or perceived, fuels the emotional loyalty that binds them to Trump. The past he seeks to restore may be idealized or selectively remembered, but it resonates powerfully.

Trump also personalizes this **grievance politics**. He claims that attacks on him are attacks on his supporters. When he is investigated, criticized, or indicted, he tells his base: "They're not after me—they're after you." This rhetoric of shared grievance strengthens the emotional bond and makes it even harder for followers to step away, even in the face of evidence or scandal[11].

This approach is effective because it provides a simple explanation for complex frustrations. It reframes economic and social changes as part of a broader moral and cultural struggle. It fosters tribal thinking and loyalty through a shared sense of persecution, while discouraging complexity or compromise.

Addressing this dynamic requires more than facts. Economic reforms and honest political engagement are essential—but so is acknowledging the emotional component. Ignoring the real fears that fuel Trump's appeal only allows grievance politics to fester.

"Us-versus-Them" Mentality and Tribal Reinforcement

Trump's rhetoric often emphasizes a strong **us-versus-them** dynamic, where his supporters see themselves as patriots battling a corrupt elite, liberal activists, and dishonest media. This binary worldview turns criticism into a personal attack, and reinforces loyalty even in the face of damning facts.

This kind of **black-and-white thinking** is a hallmark of political tribalism. As journalist Anne Applebaum explains in *Twilight of Democracy*[12], "Authoritarians tell their followers that they are victims of dangerous enemies, that only they can protect them, and that compromise is treason." In Trump's world, you're either with him or against him. His rhetoric frames opponents as existential threats to the nation[13]. This framing shifts political discourse from debate to warfare, and turns loyalty into a moral obligation.

Trump frequently depicts his followers as an embattled group under siege. Immigrants, Democrats, the press, and even Republican critics are portrayed as threats to American values[14]. This recurring crisis-oriented framing ensures that his base remains emotionally engaged and aligned.

One tactic Trump uses to reinforce this division is **demonizing the opposition**. He frequently uses derisive nicknames—"Crooked Hillary," "Sleepy Joe," "Pocahontas"—that reduce opponents to caricatures. He characterizes major media outlets like CNN and *The New York Times* as "fake news" or "enemies of the people," discrediting information that contradicts his narrative.

Trump also presents himself as a victim of political persecution. Each impeachment, indictment, or investigation becomes another chapter in the narrative of political persecution. He positions himself as a martyr, and by extension, his followers see themselves as martyrs too. The line "I'm just in the way—they're after you" exemplifies this strategy[15].

Social identity theory explains why this works. When people strongly identify with a group, they trust in-group members and view outsiders with suspicion. This **in-group bias** means Trump's base rejects criticism and clings to loyalty—not as political preference, but as self-preservation[16].

The consequences of this mentality are dangerous. It erodes trust in democratic institutions, discourages compromise, and raises the risk of political violence. Events like the January 6th Capitol attack were fueled by this logic: if the system is rigged and the enemy is evil, then breaking the rules becomes a form of heroism.

Undoing this kind of tribalism requires more than polite disagreement. It demands systemic efforts to rebuild trust, encourage dialogue, and promote shared values. Without these, polarization will deepen, and democracy will continue to erode[17].

The "Stolen Election" Narrative and Trump's Scandal Immunity

Perhaps the most telling example of Trump's enduring grip is the "stolen election" narrative. Despite over 60 court rulings rejecting fraud claims, bipartisan certifications of the results, and even testimony under oath of Trump's own appointees, millions still believe he won in 2020[18].

This false belief didn't emerge spontaneously—it was carefully cultivated. Months before the election, Trump claimed mail-in ballots were fraudulent. After losing, he escalated his claims into conspiracy theories, amplified by Right-wing media and social platforms. His legal team's lawsuits, though consistently dismissed by the courts for offering no evidence, gave the illusion of legitimacy.

Like other conspiracy theories, the stolen election claim is self-reinforcing. Evidence disproving fraud is dismissed as part of the cover-up. Judges, election officials, and Republicans who upheld the results are labeled traitors. The more it's disproven, the more believers see it as being suppressed—proof that it must be true.

Trump's immunity to scandal is a defining feature of his political resilience. From the *Access Hollywood* tape[19] to hush money payments, from financial fraud to multiple criminal indictments, none have weakened his base. That's because Trump doesn't just deny wrongdoing—he reframes it as persecution. In *Stronger Than Truth*[20], author Steven Hassan writes, "Criticism of the leader—even when based on clear facts—is reframed as persecution. The more the leader is attacked, the more devoted the followers become."

By saying "they're not after me—they're after you," Trump transfers accountability from himself to his supporters. Every investigation becomes a badge of honor; every indictment, another attack by a corrupt system.

Selective media consumption reinforces this. Fox News, Newsmax, and OANN downplay or distort the implications of Trump's legal problems. In this media echo chamber, disconfirming evidence is ignored, and pro-Trump narratives dominate. Scandals are routinely reframed as either overblown or fabricated.

Scandal fatigue[21,22,23] also plays a role. With so many controversies, none sticks. The constant cycle of outrage desensitizes the public. What would be career-ending for most politicians becomes white noise for Trump. Each new revelation is absorbed into the narrative of persecution.

Trump's enduring appeal isn't just fueled by misinformation. It's about emotional investment, shared identity, and a sense of belonging. For many, Trump represents not just a candidate but a cause. Abandoning him would mean rejecting part of themselves.

Conclusion: Beyond the Facts

Understanding why people believe Trump requires more than pointing out lies. His support is not about accuracy—it's about identity, grievance, and belonging. He offers validation to the forgotten, protection to the threatened, and clarity to the overwhelmed.

Countering his influence demands more than fact-checking. It requires building a society where people feel acknowledged and protected, with a stake in the future. That means improving economic opportunity, strengthening civic education, and creating inclusive narratives that don't rely on scapegoats.

Unless those deeper emotional and psychological forces are acknowledged and addressed, Trump's appeal will persist—not because his claims are credible, but because they feel true to those who see themselves reflected in him.

And as truth gives way to narrative, and identity outweighs evidence, the danger extends beyond one man. As historian Timothy Snyder warns in *On Tyranny*[24], "Post-truth is pre-fascism. When we give up on truth, we concede power to those with the wealth and charisma to create spectacle in its place."

If we fail to confront this shift—not just politically but culturally—we risk trading democracy for something far more dangerous: an illusion of clarity delivered by those who thrive on division.

And in today's political landscape, that illusion is often manufactured and maintained not just by politicians—but by the media itself. The next chapter examines how hyper-partisan outlets and digital platforms have become key players in the spectacle, shaping not only what people believe, but *how* they come to believe it.

Chapter 10

The Media's Role in Shaping Political Ignorance

The media is often called the *fourth estate*—an independent check on power essential to a functioning democracy[1]. In its ideal form, journalism serves as a safeguard against corruption, a bridge between institutions and the public, and a source of shared understanding in a pluralistic society.

But when that institution becomes partisan, profit-driven, or complicit in disinformation, It abandons its duty to educate, choosing instead to manipulate and shield power from scrutiny. In today's media landscape, misinformation is not merely the result of careless journalism—it is often the product of deliberate editorial decisions, emotional manipulation, and financial incentives.

This critique is not aimed at all media, but specifically at hyper-partisan outlets—primarily the deceptively-named Fox News, and other smaller Right-wing sources of misinformation their audiences mistake for legitimate news.

The consequences of this distortion are profound. When citizens cannot agree on basic facts—or no longer trust the institutions that provide them—democracy itself is imperiled. Truth becomes fragmented, and perception is shaped not by evidence but by allegiance.

This chapter examines how specific segments of the media—particularly hyper-partisan Right-wing media and algorithm-driven social media platforms—have contributed to widespread political ignorance and tribalism through disinformation campaigns. While all media ecosystems have flaws, some are not just flawed, but structured to mislead and sustain corruption. And in the United States, this distortion has become not just a byproduct of polarization—but a driving force behind it.

The Shift from Journalism to Sensationalism

Once dominated by the "big three" television networks, the media landscape has splintered into a complex web of cable networks, websites, influencers, podcasts, and social media feeds. The 24-hour news cycle, pioneered by CNN in the 1980s, fueled an insatiable demand for constant content. Fact-checking declined, speculation increased, and sensationalism took center stage[2].

Fox News, launched in 1996, changed the game entirely. Marketed as "fair and balanced," it positioned itself as a conservative alternative to mainstream media, tapping into longstanding grievances among conservatives who felt unheard and dismissed. In reality, Fox created a new standard for **ideologically driven reporting**, offering not balance, but tribal validation.

Unlike traditional outlets striving for objectivity, Fox blurred the line between news and opinion. Anchors like Sean Hannity and Tucker Carlson made no pretense of neutrality. Rather than inform viewers, they reinforced confirmation bias, supplying narratives that aligned with viewers' preexisting beliefs. Over time, this led to a siloed audience—highly engaged, fiercely loyal, and deeply misinformed.

This model has been highly profitable. In today's attention economy, media companies measure success by engagement—clicks and shares—not accuracy. Fox mastered this approach, packaging complex issues into emotionally resonant stories that spark fear, anger, and loyalty.

The Fox News Effect

Numerous studies[3,4] have documented the **Fox News effect**—the measurable impact that consuming Right-wing media has on viewers' understanding of reality. Regular Fox viewers are more likely to believe the 2020 election was stolen, that climate change is a hoax, and that COVID vaccines are dangerous. This is not incidental—it is the result of **intentional narrative shaping**.

In 2023, internal documents from the Dominion Voting Systems defamation lawsuit revealed that Fox executives and hosts knowingly aired false claims about election fraud—not because they believed them, but because they feared losing viewers to even more extreme outlets like Newsmax and OANN[5]. Hosts admitted privately that Trump's claims were nonsense, even as they platformed guests promoting them nightly.

This level of deception isn't a "both sides" issue. Mainstream outlets make mistakes, but they typically correct them and face accountability. Fox, by contrast, continues to promote false narratives even after they've been thoroughly debunked. Their business model depends on sustaining crisis and victimhood.

The consequences are real. Research shows[6] that viewers of Fox News are less informed—not just misinformed—on key public policy issues. In one study, participants who stopped watching Fox for just a month showed notable shifts in their factual understanding and political views.

The network doesn't just present the news—it constructs a worldview in which one party is always under siege and the other is evil. As Brian Stelter writes in *Network of Lies*[6], "Fox didn't just cover the news—it built an alternate reality, a place where facts bent to fit the narrative and dissenting voices were cast as enemies."

This form of storytelling creates **informational captivity**. Fox doesn't just tell viewers what to think—it tells them what to *fear*, and whom to *blame*. This breeds tribalism, distorts reality, and undermines trust in institutions. Once belief becomes identity, facts no longer matter.

Liberal Media: Not Immune, but Not Equivalent

Critics often claim that left-leaning outlets like MSNBC or CNN are just as biased. There is truth to the idea that these networks tilt liberal in tone and topic selection. They too prioritize engagement, often highlight the failures of the right, and amplify cultural narratives that resonate with their audiences. As documented by Kathleen Hall Jamieson and Joseph Cappella in *Echo Chamber*[7], "Partisan media do not just offer slanted news—they alter the way audiences process political information."

However, there is a fundamental asymmetry between mainstream media and the Right-wing media ecosystem. News outlets like The New York Times, Washington Post, and PBS employ professional standards of verification, issue corrections, and draw distinctions between reporting and opinion. Their editorial boards may lean liberal, but they do not routinely fabricate stories or suppress known facts.

MSNBC, for example, has been criticized for overemphasizing the Trump-Russia story. But that is not equivalent to Fox News promoting baseless claims of voter fraud, or dismissing a pandemic as overblown while people died.

Moreover, liberal viewers tend to consume a more diverse mix of media. Studies show they are more likely to follow multiple outlets, while conservatives often rely on a single dominant source— typically Fox News[8]. The danger lies not in bias alone, but in the consolidation of narrative control[9].

Still, liberal media has its own blind spots. Progressive outlets often underplay issues that don't align with their audience's values, use loaded language, or elevate stories that confirm ideological expectations. The risk isn't fabrication—it's omission, framing, and selective amplification.

In short, both sides have bias. But only one side has built an ecosystem where disinformation is a feature, not a bug.

Social Media as a Vector for Misinformation

Social media platforms—Facebook, YouTube, X (formerly Twitter), and TikTok—play a central role in spreading political misinformation. Unlike traditional media, these platforms rely on algorithms optimized for engagement. Content that evokes strong emotions, especially outrage, gets prioritized—accuracy be damned. As Zeynep Tufekci explains in *Twitter and Tear Gas*[10], "Attention is now the scarcest commodity online, and outrage is a dependable way to capture it."

The platforms profit from this chaos. The longer users engage—clicking, liking, commenting—the more data is harvested and ads delivered. Truth, nuance, and context take a back seat to virality[12].

Disinformation campaigns thrive in this environment. From Russian troll farms to domestic conspiracy theorists, bad actors exploit algorithms to push lies[13]. A meme, a headline, or a deepfake video can reach millions before fact-checkers even respond. And even when platforms act, removal often comes too late.

The architecture of these platforms encourages ideological isolation. Algorithms reinforce prior beliefs and screen out opposing voices, enclosing users in powerful echo chambers. Over time, people become immersed in a self-validating informational cocoon[14].

Worse, content moderation efforts are often inconsistent, reactive, or politicized. When platforms label false claims or remove harmful posts, some users see it as censorship—further reinforcing belief in conspiracy theories. Others simply move to unregulated platforms like Telegram or Truth Social.

The outcome is a fragmented public square where lies travel faster than facts, and outrage is monetized. The erosion of shared reality isn't a glitch—it's the point.

Selective Exposure and Informational Closure

One of the most insidious effects of the modern media ecosystem is **selective exposure**—the tendency for individuals to seek out information that confirms their existing beliefs while avoiding contradictory perspectives. This isn't a new phenomenon, but it has been drastically intensified by personalized algorithms, filter bubbles, and self-curated media diets. As Cass Sunstein observed in *Republic: Divided Democracy in the Age of Social Media*[15], "When people isolate themselves in echo chambers, they become more extreme, more confident, and less willing to compromise."

Platforms like Facebook, YouTube, and TikTok tailor content to each user's past behavior. This is a closed loop of affirmation: users are shown what they already agree with, and opposing views are filtered out. This leads to **epistemic closure**, where people not only believe they are right, but assume it's self-evident—and that dissenters are either uninformed or acting in bad faith.

Selective exposure accelerates polarization, not only by reinforcing tribal identities, but by making genuine dialogue nearly impossible. If one's entire information environment validates only one worldview, dissent begins to feel not just misguided—but dangerous. As this feedback loop tightens, misinformation is more readily absorbed, and corrections are more easily rejected.

Local journalism—once a moderating force—is in steep decline, leaving individuals increasingly reliant on national, partisan, or algorithmically driven content. The result is an electorate divided not just by values, but by incompatible versions of reality.

Combating selective exposure requires intentional effort. Individuals must actively seek out diverse sources, question their assumptions, and remain open to dissonant information. Media literacy programs, educational reforms, and algorithmic transparency can help—but without a shared informational baseline, democratic discourse falters.

Manufactured Outrage and "Both Sides" Journalism

In the rush to appear balanced, some mainstream outlets fall into the trap of **false equivalency**—treating unequal claims as if they deserve equal weight. This "both sides" approach gives legitimacy to fringe views and distorts the perception of consensus.

When one party spreads election lies and the other affirms democratic norms, the issue is not partisan—it's factual. Yet many newsrooms avoid saying "Trump lied" and instead write, "Trump claimed, without evidence …" This hedging may seem fair, but it obscures the truth.

"Balance" becomes distortion when it elevates falsehoods. It allows bad-faith actors to manipulate coverage by flooding the media with outrageous claims. When journalists pursue neutrality at the expense of truth, they become tools of misinformation. As Brooke Gladstone warns in *The Trouble with Reality*[16], "Objectivity has become a shield for false balance. When truth becomes partisan, neutrality becomes complicity."

At the same time, outrage-based coverage—on all sides—reduces public discourse to a theater of scandal. Complex stories are flattened into clickbait. Nuance is lost. Every controversy becomes a crisis, and real accountability is replaced by performative indignation.

This has eroded public trust. Many now view the media as hopelessly partisan or fatally incompetent.[17]. According to Gallup, trust in mass media to report the news fully, accurately, and fairly is near record lows—especially among conservatives[18]. This vacuum is filled by conspiracy theories and fringe voices[19].

The Need for Media Literacy and Structural Reform

Combating misinformation demands media literacy, platform accountability, and a recommitment to journalistic integrity.

Media literacy must start early. Students must be taught how to question sources and verify what they read, with a critical eye for bias. Understanding how algorithms shape what we see is essential in the digital age.

Journalism must also change. Newsrooms need to distinguish clearly between reporting and commentary, resist false equivalence and reinvest in investigative journalism. Corrections must be timely and visible. The goal should be truth—not clicks.

Social media platforms must be held accountable. Algorithmic transparency, independent oversight, and stronger content moderation policies are vital. Profit should not come at the expense of democracy.

Finally, the public must demand better. Supporting credible journalism, rejecting sensationalism, and resisting tribal narratives is not just a personal responsibility—it's a civic one.

The media can still serve as a bulwark against disinformation—but only if we demand it.

Yet not all outlets aim to inform. Some, like Fox News, have consciously chosen a different path. In court filings and public statements, Fox has defined itself not as a journalistic enterprise, but as an entertainment brand. Its goal isn't to report facts—it's to satisfy an audience—keeping viewers emotionally engaged, politically loyal, and constantly outraged.

In this environment, truth becomes optional. Corrections are rare, commentary blurs with reporting, and misinformation is a strategy. The abandonment of journalistic standards isn't accidental; it's an adaptation to a media economy where tribalism sells and accountability alienates the base.

The next chapter explores how hyper-partisan outlets—and Fox in particular—emerged as the linchpin of a media ecosystem built on misinformation and tribal identity—and why its influence poses a unique threat to democratic discourse.

Chapter 11

The Role of Fox and Hyper-Partisan Media

The rise of partisan media—especially Fox News—has profoundly reshaped American political perception. No longer just a right-leaning alternative, Fox has positioned itself as a dominant cultural force—trading journalism for entertainment, and facts for narrative.

Once framed as a news outlet, it now functions as a propaganda engine: amplifying misinformation, reinforcing tribal identity, and shielding political power from accountability. Its influence reaches far beyond its viewership—shaping what Republican leaders say, what voters believe, and how reality is perceived.

This chapter examines how financial incentives, ideological commitments, and high-profile personalities transformed Fox into a central pillar of the conservative movement—and a key driver of political ignorance.

The Economics of Hyper-Partisanship

As previously noted, Fox News was founded as a conservative counterweight to what was perceived as liberal media bias[1]. Over time, the network's programming shifted from ideological emphasis to overt partisan advocacy. This evolution was not merely philosophical—it was driven by economics.

Fox's business model depends on a loyal, highly engaged conservative audience[2]. Unlike traditional outlets that appeal to a politically diverse viewership, Fox maximizes revenue by delivering emotionally charged content that confirms its audience's beliefs. As journalist Matt Taibbi writes in *Hate Inc.*[3], "Outrage is a business model. The news isn't there to inform you. It's there to confirm your prejudices and keep you coming back for more."

Outrage and fear generate more engagement than balance or nuance—and that engagement fuels ad revenue, cable subscriptions, and Fox Nation's digital growth[4].

This audience-centric model leaves little room for deviation. When Fox briefly acknowledged Joe Biden's 2020 victory, viewership dropped sharply—and the network quickly pivoted to amplify election fraud narratives. The message was unmistakable: even brief honesty could cost Fox its most loyal viewers.

The threat of competition has only reinforced this trend. In *The OANN Effect*[5], journalist Max Ball notes, "The rise of fringe competitors like Newsmax and OANN didn't just echo Fox—they forced it to go further, faster, into ideological extremism."

As smaller networks like Newsmax and OANN adopted even more extreme rhetoric, they pushed Fox further into ideological territory to keep its audience from defecting. This feedback loop—between the demands of its radicalized audience and the network's pursuit of profit—has entrenched Fox in a model where misinformation is not an accident, but a strategy. As Brian Stelter observes in *Network of Lies*[6], "Fox wasn't just chasing ratings—it was building a worldview. One where facts were malleable and loyalty was everything."

Crucially, Fox doesn't claim to be a traditional news organization. It defines itself as an entertainment network—allowing it to sidestep journalistic norms while maintaining a loyal audience who believes they are watching real news.

The Influence of Fox's Primetime Hosts

Fox News' primetime lineup—Tucker Carlson, Sean Hannity, and Laura Ingraham—has done more to shape conservative opinion than any elected official in the past two decades. As media scholar Marc Rosenwald argues in *Hostile Takeover*[7], "These aren't journalists—they're ideological entrepreneurs who shape the narrative of the American Right with more influence than Congress itself."

Tucker Carlson brought intellectual style to radical talking points, normalizing conspiracy theories like the "Great Replacement"—the idea that political elites are engineering demographic change to undermine white voters[8]. His polished delivery masks xenophobic and authoritarian ideas in populist rhetoric, offering viewers a justification to embrace beliefs they might otherwise reject.

Sean Hannity functioned as a near-extension of the Trump administration, even reportedly advising Trump directly. He repeatedly echoed unsubstantiated claims about election fraud, government conspiracies, and liberal treachery. His role blurred any remaining line between media and politics.

Laura Ingraham focused on cultural grievances, routinely attacking progressive movements, health mandates, and immigration reform. She casts Democrats as existential threats to traditional values, pushing her audience into a constant state of cultural alarm. Stelter writes in *Hoax*[9], "Fox's primetime was less a news show than a nightly affirmation ritual, reinforcing what its viewers already believed and feared."

These hosts don't inform—they construct an **alternate reality**. Democrats are framed not as opponents, but as enemies. Institutions are depicted as corrupt. Their audience is conditioned to believe that only Fox tells the truth, and that everyone else— mainstream media, scientists, judges, even former Republican leaders—is part of a vast plot to destroy "real America" [10].

This messaging has tangible consequences. Fox's embrace of the stolen election lie fueled the January 6th insurrection. Its downplaying of COVID-19 and undermining of public health measures correlated with lower vaccination rates and higher mortality among conservatives. These aren't abstract harms— they're real-world outcomes of partisan media.

When challenged in court, Fox argues that its hosts are entertainers whose statements should not be taken literally. Yet audiences take them seriously, treating their commentary as gospel. This legal dodge enables misinformation to be disseminated on a massive scale with no accountability.

The Dominion Lawsuit: A Glimpse Behind the Curtain

In 2023, Fox agreed to pay $787.5 million to settle a defamation lawsuit brought by Dominion Voting Systems. The suit alleged that Fox knowingly promoted false claims about Dominion's role in election fraud—claims that were instrumental in radicalizing viewers after the 2020 election.

What made the case especially damning were internal messages revealed during litigation. Carlson and Hannity privately mocked the fraud narrative, calling Trump's legal team "insane" and the allegations "absurd". Producers and executives admitted the claims were baseless—yet they allowed them to air, fearing a ratings dip if they told the truth.

Despite the size of the settlement, Fox made no on-air apology and issued no formal retraction. Most viewers never saw the internal contradictions between what Fox was saying publicly and what it admitted privately. Instead of changing course, the network simply moved on to new grievances.

This pattern—mislead, deny, deflect—is at the heart of Fox's strategy. When Rupert Murdoch was asked why Fox continued to air conspiracy theories and disinformation, he replied, "green". The Dominion lawsuit confirmed what critics had long suspected: Fox knowingly prioritized profit and viewer loyalty over truth. As journalist Margaret Sullivan notes in *Ghosting the News*[11], "When news becomes a product and outrage becomes the pitch, truth is the first casualty."

Even after such a high-profile settlement, Fox's core audience remains loyal. Most dismiss the lawsuit as politically motivated, underscoring just how deep the ideological insulation runs. Other defamation suits, like the one filed by Smartmatic, are ongoing— but unless Fox loses its audience, there will be little pressure to change.

When Entertainment Disguises Itself as Journalism

Fox's success lies in its ability to present entertainment as news. Though its primetime content consists almost entirely of opinion and commentary, many viewers consider it a trustworthy journalistic source. And that confusion is intentional.

True journalism prioritizes verification, skepticism, and accountability. It draws a clear line between fact and opinion. Fox blurs that line deliberately. Its primetime hosts rely on selective framing, inflammatory language, and **outrage cycles** to keep audiences engaged and emotionally invested.

The network's former hard news division has been dismantled or marginalized. What remains is a media machine that packages partisan narratives as news, without adhering to the standards of responsible reporting.

By framing every issue as a crisis—whether immigration, public health, or education—Fox keeps its viewers in a constant state of alarm, tightening their emotional bond to the network. This sense of crisis discourages critical thinking and fosters tribalism.

It's not that Fox viewers are unintelligent—it's that they're being systematically misled. The network's tactics are emotionally manipulative: they create a cycle in which fear fuels loyalty, loyalty reinforces belief, and belief blinds viewers to evidence.

The result is **epistemic closure**—a worldview so tightly sealed that facts cannot penetrate it. Fox doesn't just mold opinion; it creates reality. In *The Constitution of Knowledge*[12], Jonathan Rauch writes, "A closed belief system, once established, does not merely resist correction—it turns correction into evidence of persecution."

Conclusion

Fox News isn't just a partisan outlet—it's become a central institution within the conservative movement, shaping political identities and driving national discourse. By presenting narrative as news and opinion as truth, it has fostered a culture of mistrust, fear, and ideological isolation.

Fox's influence extends beyond its core audience. Its talking points are echoed by Republican leaders, amplified by mainstream media, and absorbed by millions of voters.

Countering this influence is not easy. Media literacy can help audiences recognize propaganda. Legal consequences, like the Dominion settlement, may expose internal hypocrisy. But ultimately, the solution lies in rebuilding a culture that values truth over tribalism. Until then, partisan media will continue to sell outrage for profit and warp democracy in the process.

And as the network amplifies emotion over evidence, loyalty over logic, and spectacle over substance, it doesn't just shape what people think—it helps determine *who* they follow. That influence extends deep into the Republican Party, where media-driven narratives now drive electoral strategy, suppress dissent, and redefine what it means to lead.

But that shift in leadership didn't happen by accident. Over the past two decades, the GOP has undergone a fundamental transformation—from a coalition of ideas to a machinery of loyalty and performance. The next chapter explores how party leaders embraced spectacle, grievance, and disinformation not just to reflect the media environment, but to compete—and survive—within it.

Chapter 12

How Political Figures Manipulate Their Base

Many Republican leaders have adapted to this new political reality by knowingly spreading misinformation and weaponizing fear to maintain power. Rather than engage in substantive policy debates, today's GOP relies on loyalty tests, cultural grievance, and a feedback loop with Right-wing media.

These choices don't reflect intellectual decline—they're tactics. The goal isn't to persuade, but to mobilize followers, distract from failures, and assert dominance.

This isn't a fringe tactic—it's become the party's dominant operating principle. Performative outrage replaces governance. Emotional appeal outweighs evidence.

As Tom Nichols observes in *The Death of Expertise*[1], "Political ignorance isn't just a problem—it's a strategy. When leaders demand loyalty over knowledge, they're not just bypassing debate; they're dismantling democracy."

This chapter explores how the party shifted from traditional conservatism to personality-driven politics—and how that shift enables the manipulation of its base.

From Conservatism to Cult of Personality

The Republican Party once championed limited government, fiscal responsibility, and free markets. But those guiding principles have been replaced by an overarching requirement: loyalty to Donald Trump.

This shift is starkly visible in the party's silence— even complicity—when Trump's actions conflict with conservative values. His anti-NATO rhetoric, trade wars, admiration for autocrats, and soaring deficits would once have been disqualifying[2]. Now, they're tolerated—or even embraced. Figures like Liz Cheney and Adam Kinzinger have been pushed out, while performative loyalty is rewarded with leadership and airtime[3].

Ideological coherence no longer matters. What matters is staying on script. As David Corn writes in *American Psychosis*[4], "The Republican Party has become so consumed by its own mythology that deviation from the script is treated not as dissent—but as betrayal." Republican lawmakers who challenge Trump risk public condemnation, primary challenges, or exile from the party. Their survival now depends on amplifying Trump's grievances and attacking perceived enemies—be it immigrants, journalists, or their own colleagues.

This shift has also reshaped GOP electoral strategy. Rather than expanding their appeal, party leaders double down on energizing their most extreme factions, framing each election as an existential struggle. The legislative focus has narrowed to culture war battles like banning books, attacking LGBTQ+ rights, and targeting immigration—issues designed to provoke outrage rather than solve problems.

The GOP has become a personality cult. Policy expertise is devalued. Rational discourse is dismissed. What matters is repetition of approved narratives, and performance over governance.

Fear as a Political Weapon

Fear is one of the most effective tools in political persuasion—and Republican leaders have perfected its use. By framing opposition as a threat to traditional America, they bypass critical thinking and activate tribal identity.

The GOP tells voters that their way of life is under siege. Cultural changes—immigration, racial justice, LGBTQ+ rights—are portrayed not as progress or debate but as existential threats. These fears are emotionally potent and feed a powerful us-versus-them mentality. In *How Fascism Works*[5], Jason Stanley explains, "Authoritarian leaders cultivate a sense of victimhood among their base, framing all progress as an attack on a mythologized past."

Crime, too, is politicized. Right-wing leaders and media amplify crimes in Democratic-led cities, regardless of broader trends, to stoke a sense of lawlessness.[6,7,8]. These narratives often carry racial undertones and reinforce stereotypes aimed at galvanizing older, white voters.

Foreign threats—China, illegal immigration, globalist institutions—are folded into the same emotional script. Vague dangers are tied to personal anxieties. Fear—of invasion, of elite betrayal, or of losing control—fuels a siege mentality[9]. Voters are told they're the last line of defense.

Elections are now portrayed as zero-sum. If Republicans lose, it's not democracy—it's theft. By preemptively claiming fraud, leaders justify any outcome and delegitimize opposition victories.

Fear isn't a byproduct—it's a strategy. Per journalist Peter Pomerantsev in *This Is Not Propaganda*[10], "Authoritarian propaganda isn't about convincing—it's about creating a sense of helplessness, of a world so rigged that resistance feels futile."

Right-wing media thrives on sensationalism. Politicians benefit from crisis narratives. The result is a base that's anxious, emotionally committed, and resistant to alternative views.

In this environment, fear replaces policy. Leaders need not offer solutions—only enemies. As Cathy Young explains in *Wrong*[11], "In hyper-partisan media environments, truth is no longer a shared standard—it becomes a partisan weapon, reshaped to fit the emotional needs of the audience."

When narratives are built on fear rather than fact, persuasion gives way to performance. The aim is no longer to inform—but to provoke—ensuring the audience feels anger, threat, and urgency, even when no crisis exists.

High-Profile Manipulations: The "Big Lie," Project 2025, and January 6

Three episodes show how GOP leaders weaponize misinformation to reshape perception and maintain control: the Big Lie, Project 2025, and January 6.

The Big Lie

After the 2020 election, Donald Trump and his allies promoted the false claim that the election was stolen. Despite dozens of court rulings, bipartisan certifications, and rejected lawsuits, the GOP continued to amplify the lie—because it worked.

This wasn't just Trump's lie—it became the party's narrative. GOP leaders knew it was false but saw political gain. Candidates embraced election denial to earn Trump's endorsement. Republican-led legislatures passed new voter restrictions under the guise of "election integrity," disproportionately targeting communities of color.

Polls show a majority of Republican voters still believe the election was rigged. The "Big Lie" is now more than a conspiracy theory—it's a litmus test for party loyalty. Leaders who deny it face marginalization. Those who affirm it are rewarded with influence.

This tactic has deeply corroded trust in democracy. It encourages election denial and political violence, while casting all opposition victories as illegitimate.

Project 2025

Project 2025 is a comprehensive plan—over 900 pages—to restructure the federal government under future Republican leadership. Framed as a fix for "Deep State" overreach, it proposes replacing career civil servants with loyal political appointees, dismantling federal agencies, and centralizing power in the executive branch.

Though underreported, Project 2025 is a blueprint for authoritarian governance. It calls for purging watchdogs like Inspectors General, shutting down government publications, and eliminating departments like Education. It proposes purging thousands of scientists and public servants—especially in climate, health, and regulation—and replacing them with loyal ideologues.

The plan also outlines sweeping attacks on reproductive freedom, LGBTQ+ inclusion, and environmental safeguards. Though cloaked in the language of "liberty", these changes serve narrow ideological and corporate interests.

In the early months of Trump's return to power, many Project 2025 proposals were already in motion—via executive orders, firings, and policy shifts. It is not hypothetical. It is a strategic roadmap to subvert democratic checks and consolidate power. Barbara McQuade, in *Attack from Within*[12], warns: "Disinformation isn't just about distorting facts—it's about disabling the institutions that check abuse of power."

January 6

The January 6 attack on the U.S. Capitol was the most visible consequence of political misinformation. Trump's rhetoric, amplified by GOP leaders and Right-wing media, convinced thousands of Americans that the election was stolen—and that violence was justified.

Five people died; dozens were injured. And yet, rather than condemn the attack, many Republicans reversed course. Initial condemnation quickly gave way to revisionist narratives: they claimed the rioters were patriots and the violence overstated—some even called it a false flag.

Right-wing media, led by figures like Tucker Carlson, reframed the assault as peaceful protest. Elected officials echoed these narratives. Investigations were blocked or delegitimized. Trump promised to pardon many of the rioters, and GOP lawmakers followed suit.

January 6 is now celebrated in some corners of the right. Convicted rioters are called "political prisoners." The insurrection has been normalized—and even valorized—as part of the ongoing "battle" for American values. In *How Democracies Die*[13], Levitsky and Ziblatt write: "When political violence is tolerated, and even rewarded, democratic norms begin to erode—not from without, but from within."

This normalization is dangerous. It signals that political violence is permissible—if it serves the right narrative. It undermines rule of law, encourages future extremism, and further corrodes public trust in democratic institutions.

The Feedback Loop Between GOP Leaders and Conservative Media

The weaponization of political ignorance is sustained by a feedback loop between Republican leaders and right-wing media.

Politicians make inflammatory claims. Fox News, Newsmax, and OANN amplify them. Viewers accept them as fact. Then politicians cite media coverage as validation. This circular logic turns lies into consensus.

The loop isolates voters from reality. Alternative perspectives are dismissed as "fake news." Even international outlets aligned with mainstream U.S. coverage are cast as part of a vast conspiracy. In this worldview, only conservative Americans know the "truth."

This system forces conformity. Republican leaders who step outside it are vilified. Moderates are pushed rightward. Fringe ideas become party doctrine. Even those who know the truth remain silent—because survival requires submission.

The loop doesn't just reflect public opinion—it manufactures it. It creates a system that feeds outrage and punishes dissent, all while pushing politicians toward the extreme[14]. It's a closed ecosystem, immune to correction.

And it is not benign. It lays the groundwork for conspiracy theories, institutional distrust, and political violence. When citizens are told that elections are rigged, that their opponents are criminals, and that only their party can save the country—democracy begins to erode.

Conclusion

The GOP's manipulation of its base is strategic. By abandoning traditional conservatism in favor of **personality-driven politics**, and replacing policy with fear, misinformation, and loyalty tests, the party has created an electorate primed for authoritarian solutions.

This system is sustained by Right-wing media, fueled by outrage, and safeguarded by leaders who fear political exile more than democratic collapse. The few who resist are cast out. The many who conform are complicit.

Breaking this cycle demands media reform, civic education, structural accountability, and a renewed commitment to truth as a public good[15].

The next chapter explores how even Republican leaders—once architects of this system—have become its prisoners, unable to escape the trap they helped build. What began as a strategy to manipulate others has become a structure that manipulates them. And in that system, the cost of honesty isn't just criticism—it's exile.

Chapter 13

The Echo Chamber of Republican Leadership

Today's Republican leadership operates inside the same misinformation ecosystem that misleads its base. What began as calculated manipulation has become a closed loop—where party officials are shaped by the very forces they once sought to control, including Right-wing media, radicalized primary voters, and pressure from within their own ranks.

This chapter explores how conservative media now dictates party priorities, how the line between strategy and belief has blurred, and how electoral structures like primary elections have locked the GOP into its own echo chamber.

When Media Becomes the Master

The relationship between conservative media and Republican leadership has inverted. Once a tool for message amplification, media platforms like Fox News, Newsmax, and OANN now enforce party orthodoxy.

GOP leaders no longer lead the conversation—they chase it. This trend was documented early on by David Brock, who detailed how conservative media was built not to reflect GOP messaging, but to define it[1]. As Brian Klaas writes in *The Despot's Accomplice*[2], "When political leaders outsource their agenda to demagogues and media provocateurs, they stop leading—and start echoing."

Deviation from core narratives—particularly around election legitimacy and Trump's authority—is swiftly condemned, often orchestrated through media personalities who shape the views of the party's base. Even moderate Republicans are forced to fall in line or face political exile. Data show that much of the GOP base consumes multiple conservative outlets like Fox News and Newsmax, creating redundancy and reinforcing ideological conformity[3]. This media saturation makes it nearly impossible for dissenting perspectives to break through—leaders are not just echoing the base; they are immersed in the same information environment.

Fact-based policymaking has given way to soundbites and culture war skirmishes. Today's GOP leaders court appearances on conservative programs as fervently as they once pursued legislative victories. Getting airtime on Hannity or Breitbart may matter more than passing legislation.

This dynamic reflects Trump's political style, where "good TV" trumps good governance. Fox personalities and podcast influencers often hold more sway than party elders or committee chairs. The result is a Republican leadership team that doesn't just use media—it is shaped by it.

Cynics and True Believers

Not all Republican leaders relate to misinformation in the same way. Some are **cynical manipulators**, who knowingly spread falsehoods to maintain power. Others are **true believers**, who've internalized the conspiracy theories they once deployed as tools.

Figures like Mitch McConnell or Kevin McCarthy have walked the line between public allegiance and private skepticism. Leaked communications reveal a recognition of Trump's election lies—yet they continued to endorse those claims for strategic reasons.

By contrast, politicians like Marjorie Taylor Greene and Paul Gosar appear to fully inhabit the alternate reality promoted by Right-wing media. Their rhetoric isn't just performative—it reflects deeply held ideological views rooted in conspiracy and grievance, often bordering on apocalyptic nationalism.

This mix creates a dangerous instability. Cynics assumed they could control the narrative. But as true believers gained influence—and voter loyalty— they found themselves parroting the very myths they once helped construct. Otherwise, they risk being outflanked and labeled as traitors to the cause.

Nowhere is this clearer than with election denialism. In *After the Fall*[4], Ben Rhodes notes, "The real danger isn't just the lie—it's the infrastructure built around it: the politicians, platforms, and profit models that turn fiction into civic identity." Initially embraced as a temporary tool to appease Trump and his base, it is now a pillar of GOP identity, with no exit ramp for those who know it's a lie. Admitting the truth risks political suicide. This behavior reflects broader tactics outlined in the authoritarian playbook—using media and legislative levers to entrench power while undermining truth[5].

This collision of cynical strategy and sincere belief has created a party where misinformation is no longer a tactic—it is a worldview.

Primary Elections and the Incentive to Radicalize

The extremism within GOP leadership is reinforced structurally through primary elections. In many Republican districts, general elections are irrelevant; the real battle is in the primary—where turnout is low, and the most ideologically driven and uncompromising voters dominate.

To survive, candidates must appeal to the base: a base that consumes hyper-partisan media and prizes loyalty over integrity. Moderation is not just discouraged—it is punished. Even rational incumbents adopt radical rhetoric to avoid being "primaried" by challengers further to the right. Research has shown that gerrymandered districts and low-turnout primaries structurally incentivize such extremism[6,7,8].

This dynamic doesn't just shape rhetoric—it dictates behavior. Lawmakers sponsor bills on culture war issues like banning books or restricting trans athletes rather than tackling actual policy needs—not because of legislative necessity, but because such issues score points in primary debates and on social media. Manufactured outrage becomes political currency, displacing actual governance.

The consequence is a brain drain from the Republican Party. Thoughtful, pragmatic politicians are replaced by bomb-throwers who treat public office as a platform for outrage performance. Those who remain often suppress their misgivings to avoid being labeled as disloyal. Research suggests that recruiting moderate candidates with better career incentives could help reverse this trend[9].

Unless the primary system is reformed—or until extremist candidates begin consistently losing general elections—the cycle of radicalization will continue[10]. According to Ezra Klein in *Why We're Polarized*[11], "Primary elections reward extremism because they attract the most ideologically motivated voters—those most likely to punish compromise and prize performative conflict."

GOP leaders are trapped by their own voters, unable to pivot even when they recognize the damage being done.

The Broader Costs of the GOP Echo Chamber

The consequences of this feedback loop extend far beyond campaigns and media cycles—they affect governance and public trust—undermining long-term national stability.

Bipartisanship has become politically toxic. Even widely supported policies—such as infrastructure investment or public health measures—are rejected if they appear to benefit Democrats. Gridlock isn't a byproduct—it's the goal. Obstruction becomes the point.

Legislative paralysis is compounded by policy distortion. Rather than address urgent crises like healthcare affordability or climate resilience, GOP lawmakers prioritize performative hearings and partisan stunts. Governing is replaced by grievance theater.

The echo chamber also distances the party from public opinion. As journalist Marc Rosenwald put it[12], Fox has become a 'shadow caucus' for the GOP, setting agendas and punishing dissent from its televised pulpit. *In The Chaos Machine*[13], Max Fisher writes, "Digital echo chambers don't just radicalize individuals—they reshape entire institutions by feeding distorted realities back into decision-making processes."

While most Americans reject election fraud claims and culture war extremism, GOP leaders remain tethered to themes that resonate only with their radicalized base. This creates a disconnect that increasingly undermines Republican competitiveness in national elections—even as it strengthens their grip in gerrymandered districts.

Most dangerously, the echo chamber normalizes political violence. Opponents are not framed as rivals but as threats to the nation. Calls to pardon the Capitol rioters, discredit elections, and even call for dismantling federal law enforcement are no longer fringe—they are part of mainstream GOP messaging.

The idea that political violence might be justified to "save the country" is gaining traction among segments of the right. Leaders who once flirted with this rhetoric for effect now find themselves unable—or unwilling—to condemn it. The guardrails of democracy are eroding, and the GOP's refusal to confront misinformation only hastens that erosion. Historian Ruth Ben-Ghiat warns in *Strongmen: Mussolini to the Present*[14], "Authoritarians don't need to win over everyone—they need only normalize the unacceptable and silence the rest."

Conclusion

The Republican Party is no longer simply using misinformation as a tool—it has become embedded in it. Conservative media now sets the agenda, enforced by radicalized primary voters. Politicians—whether cynical or sincere—reinforce the cycle. The result is a party unmoored from democratic norms, practical policy, and even its own legacy.

Breaking the echo chamber will require bold action: reforming primaries, reshaping media incentives, and restoring a commitment to truth. Legal scholars and reform advocates have proposed structural guardrails to counter extremism[15]. Without them, the party will continue down a path of radicalization—with consequences that extend far beyond its base.

As noted previously, weaponized ignorance is not confined to the right. But in this moment, the institutional collapse of the GOP presents a uniquely dangerous challenge to American democracy.

Confronting it requires clarity, courage, and sustained effort. The chapters in Part Four offer strategies for doing just that.

Part Four: Breaking Free from Ignorance

In this final Part, we turn from diagnosis to action. Having explored how political ignorance is manufactured, spread, and sustained, we now ask: *What can be done about it?* How do we respond to a system that rewards falsehood and punishes dissent, using misinformation to divide?

Rebuilding trust in truth is no small task. But it begins with the recognition that ignorance is not inevitable. While many of the challenges are structural and long-term—requiring reform in education, media, and politics—there are also immediate steps individuals can take. Personal conversations, better media habits, and sharper critical thinking all have the potential to make a difference.

Part Four offers practical strategies applicable both to institutions and to individuals navigating a world awash in misinformation. The goal is not perfection, but progress: cultivating habits of critical thinking and media discernment, while maintaining respectful engagement with others. These tools can help people resist manipulation, counter harmful narratives, and rebuild the trust that democracy depends on. While systemic reform is essential, lasting change often starts with everyday choices and conversations—with citizens willing to question, learn, and lead by example.

The chapters in Part Four explore:

- The power of critical thinking to resist manipulation
- How media literacy can reduce susceptibility to disinformation
- Productive ways to engage with those caught in misinformation loops
- The role of education, civic discourse, and shared facts in revitalizing democracy

Many of these solutions are incremental, and some may feel slow or inadequate in the face of rising authoritarianism. But change doesn't begin at the top—it begins with people. Individuals who learn to learn to reflect and question dominant narratives—even when they appeal to tribal instincts—can spark ripple effects within their communities. Helping even one person break free from politically sponsored ignorance can be the first step toward broader progress.

Ultimately, this final Part is not just about policy or pedagogy—it's about hope. The same forces that shape belief can be redirected toward truth and reason as foundations for a renewed democracy.

Chapter 14

The Power of Critical Thinking

Ignorance flourishes where critical thinking is absent—where emotion overrides evidence, and convenience replaces curiosity. The spread of misinformation and the entrenchment of ideological bubbles are largely due to a lack of analytical reasoning and skepticism among the general public. This chapter explores ways to promote intellectual independence, resist misinformation, and develop habits that foster clear, rational thinking.

Teaching Skepticism and Media Literacy

The foundation of critical thinking lies in skepticism—an essential tool for evaluating information in an era of propaganda, misinformation, and media bias.

Teaching skepticism does not mean encouraging cynicism or outright dismissal of information but rather forming a habit of questioning sources, considering alternative perspectives, and verifying claims before accepting them as fact. As Carl Sagan famously wrote in *The Demon-Haunted World*[1], "It is far better to grasp the universe as it really is than to persist in delusion, however satisfying and reassuring."

A prime example of skepticism's power is the progress of science. Science is fundamentally skeptical: every proposed theory must be tested against experiment, and should predict new results. Even well-entrenched theories are subject to revision, and outright dismissal, if new data shows a discrepancy with the real world. Much of scientific progress comes from identifying flaws in current theories and uncovering the deeper principles that lead to their refinement or replacement.

Part of the issue with the public believing in and appreciating science is that they often misunderstand scientific terminology. For example, to a layperson, a 'theory' is just an idea, and one theory is good as the next. In science, on the other hand, a theory is a mathematical description of nature that has been tested and not only agrees with the real world, but predicts new discoveries. Understanding the same language is essential if meaningful communication and understanding are to succeed, as discussed in a later section.

Media literacy is one of the most effective ways to combat ignorance and misinformation. The ability to spot media bias, identify misinformation, and separate journalism from propaganda is critical for an informed electorate. Schools, workplaces, and public institutions should integrate media literacy education to ensure that individuals can navigate an increasingly complex information landscape. Kahne and Bowyer argue in *Educating for Democracy in a Digital Age*[2] that "Media literacy is not just a civic skill—it's a democratic imperative."

Practical methods for developing media literacy include fact-checking, cross-referencing sources, and recognizing emotional manipulation in media content. Encouraging individuals to analyze news sources for consistency, author credibility, and editorial bias engenders a more discerning public. Additionally, understanding the financial incentives behind media organizations—whether they prioritize profit, political influence, or ideological adherence—can help individuals contextualize the information they consume.

Beyond formal education, fostering skepticism in everyday life can empower individuals to resist manipulation. Encouraging people to ask simple but powerful questions—"Who benefits from this claim?", "What is the evidence?", "Is this opinion or fact?"— helps dismantle misinformation before it takes root. In their 2019 study[3], Pennycook and Rand found that "Individuals more likely to engage in reflective thinking are less susceptible to fake news." In *A Field Guide to Lies: Critical Thinking in the Information Age*[4], Daniel Levitin adds, "Information is only as good as our ability to evaluate it—without training in logic and probability, we are easily manipulated by rhetoric masquerading as truth."

When individuals learn to challenge their own assumptions, they become more resilient to external manipulation.

Recognizing Logical Fallacies and Manipulative Rhetoric

Many people fall prey to misinformation because they are unfamiliar with common logical fallacies and rhetorical tricks used in political discourse. Logical fallacies are errors in reasoning that can make an argument seem convincing even when it lacks substance. Politicians, media personalities, and propagandists often rely on these tactics to manipulate public opinion and distort reality.

Some of the most common logical fallacies used in disinformation campaigns include:

- **Strawman Argument**: Misrepresenting an opponent's position to make it easier to attack. Example: "Liberals want to abolish the police and let criminals roam free."

- **False Dilemma** (Black-and-White thinking): Presenting two extreme choices as the only possible options. Example: "You either support this war, or you hate America."

- **Appeal to Emotion**: Using fear, anger, or pity to override rational thinking. Example: "If you don't vote for this policy, your family will be in danger."

- **Ad Hominem Attack**: Attacking the character of a person rather than addressing their argument. Example: "You can't trust what they say about climate change—they drive a big SUV."

- **Bandwagon Fallacy**: Suggesting that because many people believe something, it must be true. Example: "Millions of people think the election was stolen—how can they all be wrong?"

Recognizing these fallacies enables individuals to dissect misleading arguments and engage in more meaningful discussions. As Cook and Lewandowsky explain in *The Debunking Handbook*[5], "Effective debunking requires providing a factual alternative and avoiding repetition of the myth." Teaching people to slow down, analyze arguments critically, and resist emotionally charged rhetoric helps to prevent them from being easily swayed by bad-faith actors.

The Importance of Exposure to Diverse Viewpoints

One of the most effective ways to counteract ignorance and misinformation is to expose individuals to diverse perspectives. The more people engage with differing viewpoints, the better they become at understanding complex issues, questioning their assumptions, and refining their own beliefs based on evidence rather than ideological conformity.

However, in today's media environment, people often remain trapped in ideological echo chambers, only consuming information that reinforces their existing beliefs. Social media algorithms, hyper-partisan news networks, and self-selection bias all reinforce this isolation. Encouraging individuals to break out of their bubbles is essential for developing intellectual independence.

Practical strategies for diversifying information intake include:

- **Following multiple news sources**: Consuming both left-leaning and right-leaning media can provide a broader perspective on any given issue.

- **Engaging in civil discourse**: Discussing political issues with people of different viewpoints—without hostility—can challenge assumptions and reveal blind spots.

- **Reading primary sources**: Instead of relying on secondhand interpretations, reading government reports, court rulings, and scientific studies can provide a more accurate understanding of major issues.

- **Practicing intellectual humility**: Being open to changing one's mind when presented with compelling evidence is a sign of strength, not weakness. Tversky and Kahneman's foundational work on heuristics[6] reminds us "The framing of information can significantly alter judgment and decision-making."

Diverse exposure does not mean accepting every argument at face value but rather engaging with ideas critically while maintaining an openness to new information. In a political environment where misinformation is rampant, the ability to engage with multiple perspectives is crucial to maintaining a well-informed citizenry.

Are We Even Speaking the Same Language?

In a world saturated with information and disinformation, it's easy to assume that public disagreement is primarily about facts. But often, we're not even using the same language. For example, words like *theory*, *research*, *freedom*, and *truth* can have radically different meanings depending on who is speaking and what ideological frame they inhabit. This **semantic drift**—whether innocent or intentional—undermines our ability to engage in rational dialogue. It turns debate into confusion, and confusion into fertile ground for ignorance.

Take the word **theory**, for example. In casual conversation, it often means a guess or a hunch: "I have a theory about why my neighbor's lights are always on." But in science, a theory is something far more robust. It is a comprehensive framework—a mathematical or conceptual model—that has been repeatedly tested and confirmed against real-world data. The theory of evolution, germ theory, and quantum theory are not wild ideas waiting to be proven. They are well-supported systems of understanding that make accurate predictions and guide further research. When people say "evolution is just a theory," they betray a fundamental misunderstanding—not just of science, but of language itself.

The same confusion applies to the word **research**. In the digital age, "doing your own research" often means watching YouTube videos or reading Reddit threads that confirm one's beliefs. But this is not research in any scientific sense.

Scientific research involves rigorous methodology, controls, reproducibility, peer review, and transparency about funding and potential biases. It is a communal effort, conducted by trained experts, often over years or decades. By contrast, individual internet "researchers" are deeply vulnerable to the very psychological biases this book explores: confirmation bias, motivated reasoning, and tribal identity signaling. They may believe they are free thinkers, but in reality, they are often just consumers of misinformation curated by algorithms.

This divergence in language creates the illusion of understanding. Two people may use the same words in a conversation—"I've done the research," "That's just a theory," "I care about freedom"—yet mean entirely different things. The first may be referring to peer-reviewed journal articles; the second, to a few blog posts or memes. Without a shared understanding of basic terms, communication breaks down. Worse, it allows bad-faith actors—political propagandists, cable news personalities, and social media influencers—to manipulate these ambiguities for gain.

The **weaponization of language** is one of the most subtle and dangerous forms of misinformation. When scientific terms are redefined or stripped of their precision, they become tools for ideological warfare. During the COVID-19 pandemic, the term "gain of function" became a flashpoint, weaponized to suggest sinister intent despite being a technical term with a specific scientific context. Likewise, "PCR test" became a political football, its complex limitations twisted into accusations of fraud. These moments didn't just reflect disagreement over policy—they reflected an epistemic rupture, where public and expert discourses no longer overlapped.

This isn't a call to police language pedantically, but to recognize when language fails us—or worse, is used against us. We live in a time when epistemic humility is rare, and epistemic authority is under attack. It is not enough to "agree on the facts" if we cannot agree on the meaning of the words used to describe those facts.

This challenge is compounded by the architecture of the internet. Search engines and social media don't reward precision—they reward emotional resonance and engagement. As a result, misinformation that uses familiar, emotionally charged language often spreads more quickly than carefully worded truth.

The phrase "do your own research" is seductive because it appeals to personal agency and autonomy. But without the tools to assess evidence, verify sources, or understand the scientific method, that phrase becomes a trapdoor into conspiracy thinking. Wineburg and McGrew found in their study of lateral reading[7] that "The best fact-checkers read less and click more—they leave the page to learn about the source."

There is also a kind of **semantic narcissism** at play, where people assume that the meanings they assign to words are universally understood or accepted. This is a hallmark of ideological bubbles, where linguistic shorthand becomes dogma. For example, in some circles, *freedom* means protection from government mandates; in others, it means access to health care, clean air, and public safety. Without acknowledging these divergent frameworks, we talk past each other. Worse, we entrench ourselves in mutual incomprehension, mistaking it for moral superiority.

This linguistic drift isn't merely a communication problem—it's an **epistemological crisis**. It leaves us vulnerable to manipulation and unable to reach consensus, even on issues with clear empirical answers. And it is particularly corrosive in a democracy, where shared understanding is the foundation for collective decision-making.

So how do we fix it? Education is one path—specifically, teaching critical thinking and media literacy with an emphasis on how scientific language differs from everyday usage. But we also need a **cultural shift**, where humility replaces certainty, and where asking, "What do you mean by that?" becomes a signal of strength rather than ignorance.

Until we begin to speak the same language—or at least recognize when we are not—our debates will remain exercises in futility. And in that confusion, ignorance will persist.

Conclusion

Critical thinking is not just an academic exercise—it is a necessary skill for navigating a world filled with propaganda, misinformation, and ideological manipulation. By teaching skepticism, recognizing manipulative rhetoric, and encouraging exposure to diverse perspectives, individuals can arm themselves against ignorance and become more resilient to misinformation.

Breaking free from ignorance requires effort, discipline, and a willingness to challenge one's own beliefs. However, the rewards—a better-informed public and a democracy less vulnerable to manipulation—are worth the struggle. As misinformation continues to shape political landscapes, critical thinking is one of the most powerful tools in preserving truth, reason, and democracy.

But individuals cannot do it alone. A society that values truth must also build the systems—educational, technological, and institutional—that support it. The next chapter explores how media literacy can become not just a personal skill, but a civic norm.

Chapter 15

Encouraging Media Literacy

The spread of misinformation and political ignorance is not just an individual failing—it's a systemic one. In a media environment driven by profit, sensationalism, and ideological bias, people often lack the structural support needed to critically evaluate the information they consume.

This chapter examines how education, technology, and institutional reform can help foster a more informed public—and how media literacy can evolve from an isolated classroom lesson into a cultural expectation.

The Role of Education in Fostering Media Literacy

Media literacy should be considered an essential skill, much like reading, writing, or basic math. As media scholar Renee Hobbs has argued[1], "Media literacy is not a luxury—it's a survival skill in the digital age, where misinformation competes directly with truth."

However, it is rarely prioritized in traditional education systems, leaving students unprepared to navigate an increasingly complex and deceptive information landscape. Integrating media literacy into school curricula at all levels—primary, secondary, and higher education—can equip individuals with critical thinking skills necessary to analyze news, advertising, and political messaging effectively.

An effective approach to teaching media literacy is training students to ask fundamental questions about the information they encounter:

- **Who is the source?** Assessing the credibility and potential bias of a news source is essential.

- **What is the purpose?** Identifying whether content is meant to inform, persuade, entertain, or manipulate can change how it is interpreted.

- **Is there supporting evidence?** Encouraging individuals to verify claims against multiple sources promotes deeper analysis and fact-checking habits.

- **Are emotional appeals being used?** Recognizing how emotional language shapes belief, helping distinguish genuine information from spin.

Beyond traditional education, lifelong media literacy programs should be accessible to adults, particularly in an era when misinformation spreads rapidly through social media. As emphasized in *Amusing Ourselves to Death*[2], Neil Postman warned decades ago that public discourse would deteriorate when serious issues were presented in entertaining formats—an insight that now applies to algorithm-driven media platforms. Government and nonprofit initiatives could promote public education campaigns designed to teach digital literacy and responsible media consumption to older generations who may not have grown up with the internet.

Additionally, workplaces and community organizations can play a role in promoting media literacy through community-led events and educational initiatives. Given the impact of misinformation on democracy, public health, and social stability, media literacy must be treated as a civic responsibility rather than just an academic subject.

Ultimately, widespread media literacy education could create a more discerning public, reducing the influence of misinformation and propaganda. However, education alone is not enough—technological solutions must also play a role in combating media manipulation.

Potential Technological Solutions: Blockchain-Based Verification and AI-Driven Credibility Scores

As misinformation becomes more sophisticated, technology must evolve to provide better tools for verifying the credibility of news sources. Several emerging technologies hold promise in this regard, offering potential solutions to help individuals assess the reliability of the information they encounter.

One of the most discussed innovations in combating misinformation is **blockchain-based**

verification systems. Blockchain is a decentralized digital ledger that records transactions across a network of computers so that the record cannot be altered retroactively without the alteration of all subsequent blocks.

In the context of news and media, blockchain could be used to create immutable records of news reports, linking content to its original source and timestamp. This would make it more difficult for bad actors to alter or fabricate stories while allowing consumers to trace the origins of information. Some projects have already experimented with decentralized news verification (such as Civil[3], Po.et[4], and PUBLIQ[5]), which aim to combine blockchain transparency with journalistic standards to counteract disinformation campaigns.

Another promising approach is **AI-driven credibility scoring**. Artificial intelligence can analyze news content, identify patterns of misinformation, and provide real-time credibility ratings for articles and sources. Some platforms are already using machine learning models to flag falsehoods and identify coordinated misinformation efforts (for example, NewsGuard[6], AdVerif.ai[7], and Google's Fact Check Tools[8]). If integrated into major search engines and social media platforms, AI tools could offer users real-time credibility assessments, curbing the viral spread of misinformation.

However, as Aviv Ovadya noted in his early warnings on digital misinformation[9], "Technology alone cannot distinguish truth from lies unless it is guided by transparent principles and accountable human judgment."

These technological solutions also raise ethical concerns. Who determines what is classified as misinformation? Could AI-driven tools be biased themselves? Might blockchain systems foster overreliance on centralized authorities to define truth? These concerns highlight the need for transparency and oversight in any technological solution aimed at combating misinformation.

At the same time, these technologies must be accessible and widely adopted to be effective. If only a small segment of the population uses credibility verification tools, their impact will be limited. Public and private stakeholders must collaborate to integrate these tools into everyday media consumption habits, ensuring that the public benefits from technological advancements in media validation and verification.

The Responsibility of Social Media and News Platforms

While individuals must develop critical thinking skills, media companies and tech platforms also bear responsibility for mitigating the spread of misinformation. Cass Sunstein, in *#Republic: Divided Democracy in the Age of Social Media*[10], underscores how algorithmic design can deepen polarization: "If people are sorted into information cocoons, they may never encounter views that challenge their own."

Social media giants such as Facebook, Twitter (now X), and YouTube have been criticized for enabling disinformation campaigns, amplifying conspiracy theories, and failing to regulate harmful content effectively. Without systemic reform, these platforms will continue to fuel the spread of misinformation.

Some proposed solutions include:

- **Stronger content moderation policies:** Social media companies must enforce stricter policies against false information while balancing concerns about free speech.

- **Algorithmic transparency:** Platforms should disclose how their recommendation algorithms prioritize content and whether they unintentionally amplify sensationalist or misleading narratives.

- **Fact-checking partnerships:** Collaborating with independent fact-checking organizations could accelerate the debunking of misinformation before it spreads widely.

- **Media literacy prompts:** Platforms could incorporate real-time prompts that encourage users to verify sources before sharing potentially misleading content.

- **Demonetizing false content:** Many purveyors of misinformation profit from online engagement. Stripping revenue from false content could discourage bad actors from spreading misleading narratives.

While social media companies have made some strides in addressing these issues, their efforts remain inconsistent and often reactionary. More accountability is needed to ensure that tech giants do not continue prioritizing user clicks rather than civic responsibility (or, at the least, <u>balance</u> these through conscious efforts). Additionally, the influence of major media outlets cannot be overlooked—cable news networks, talk radio, and online media must also be held to higher journalistic standards.

Regulation in this space is complex, as it intersects with free speech protections and corporate interests. However, greater transparency, public pressure, and independent oversight could encourage platforms and media companies to take misinformation more seriously and implement meaningful reforms.

Conclusion

Promoting media literacy requires a multifaceted approach that combines education, technology, and institutional accountability. Individuals must be equipped with the skills to evaluate information critically, while technological innovations should provide better tools for validating and verifying credible news. At the same time, media companies and social media platforms must take greater responsibility for limiting the spread of misinformation.

A well-informed public is essential for the survival of democracy. As journalist Maria Ressa warned in her Nobel Peace Prize speech[11], "Without facts, you can't have truth. Without truth, you can't have trust. Without trust, we have no shared reality, and democracy as we know it is dead."

Without widespread media literacy, society will continue to be vulnerable to propaganda, manipulation, and ideological extremism. The combination of education, technological advancements, and corporate accountability can help build a media environment that prioritizes truth over sensationalism.

Still, we shouldn't be naïve. Such efforts could take years or decades, and society must first decide these efforts are important enough to merit focused intervention. Unfortunately, government and industry seem to be moving in the opposite direction.

But even in the absence of top-down solutions, change can still begin from the ground up. The next chapter explores near-term strategies for engaging with individuals trapped in misinformation, providing practical approaches to fostering meaningful dialogue and challenging false beliefs in constructive ways.

Chapter 16

How to Have Conversations with Those Trapped in Misinformation

Simply presenting facts often fails to change minds. And while institutions struggle to act, individuals still hold power—especially in how we engage with one another.

Political misinformation is often rooted in emotional attachment and social identity, making it difficult to correct through direct confrontation. This chapter explores effective strategies for engaging with individuals who have fallen into misinformation traps, emphasizing empathy, patience, and the importance of opening dialogue rather than shutting it down.

The Importance of Empathy and Patience

Many people think that correcting misinformation is simply a matter of presenting facts. However, psychological research suggests that people often resist factual corrections when their deeply held beliefs are challenged. As neuroscientist Tali Sharot observed in her research on belief formation[1], "Facts don't win fights. Emotion, identity, and trust shape beliefs far more than logic ever could."

As previously discussed, this can trigger the backfire effect, in which individuals double down on misinformation as a way to defend their identity or worldview.

For this reason, empathy is crucial when engaging with someone who believes in misinformation. Rather than ridiculing or dismissing those views outright, it's more productive to acknowledge their concerns and understand the emotional factors driving their beliefs. People who feel attacked or shamed are less likely to reconsider their positions; they may even become more entrenched in their views.

Practicing patience is equally important. Changing minds is a process, not a single conversation. According to Brendan Nyhan, co-author of a seminal study on political misperceptions[2], "People rarely change their minds in the moment. Persuasion is often a slow process of cumulative exposure and reflection."

Expecting someone to immediately abandon a deeply held belief after hearing new information is unrealistic. Instead, the goal should be to plant seeds of doubt and encourage critical thinking over time. Repeated exposure to alternative viewpoints and credible evidence can gradually erode false beliefs, but only if the person is willing to engage in open-minded discussion. Hearing opposing views from trusted sources can gradually soften rigid beliefs.

To ensure productive conversations, it helps to:

- **Listen actively** without immediately correcting every false claim.

- **Find common ground** to establish trust before addressing misinformation.

- **Ask open-ended questions** that encourage self-reflection (e.g., "What led you to that conclusion?" or "Have you considered alternative perspectives?").

- **Avoid condescending language**, which can trigger defensiveness.

By engaging with empathy and patience, it becomes possible to create an environment where individuals feel comfortable questioning their own assumptions rather than feeling forced to defend them.

Identifying Small Cracks in Belief Systems to Open Dialogue

While direct confrontation can be counter-productive, finding small inconsistencies or contradictions in someone's beliefs can be an effective way to encourage critical thinking. After all, few people hold perfectly coherent worldviews—most belief systems contain contradictions, logical gaps, or misinterpretations of evidence. Identifying these weak points can provide opportunities to guide someone toward re-evaluating their assumptions.

A few strategies for doing this include:

- **Encouraging Socratic questioning**: Instead of arguing against misinformation outright, ask probing questions that encourage deeper reflection. Example: "If the election was rigged, why did Republican candidates win in the same states where Trump lost?"

- **Highlighting past belief changes:** Remind the person of instances where they have changed their mind before, reinforcing the idea that adapting beliefs based on new evidence is a sign of growth.

- **Using reputable sources that they already trust:** If a person is skeptical of mainstream media, citing figures or outlets they respect can be more persuasive than presenting evidence from sources they already dismiss.

- **Breaking down misinformation into smaller, more digestible parts:** Instead of confronting the entire belief system head-on, addressing one false claim at a time can avoid overwhelming the individual and increase the likelihood of reflection.

Crucially, the goal is not to "win" a conversation, but to plant doubt in a way that encourages independent reevaluation. By focusing on small cracks rather than challenging the entire belief system at once, people may become more open to rethinking their views over time. Psychologist Peter Boghossian, co-author of *How to Have Impossible Conversations*[3], emphasizes, "Asking questions gives people the space to examine their own reasoning. It's far more effective than telling them they're wrong."

Overcoming Psychological Barriers to Accepting Truth

Many people hold onto misinformation not because they lack intelligence but because of psychological factors such deep-seated biases and social pressures rooted in identity and group belonging. Understanding these barriers—which were discussed in earlier chapters—can help in designing effective interventions.

- **Cognitive Dissonance:** When people encounter evidence that contradicts their beliefs, they experience discomfort. To resolve this tension, they often dismiss the evidence rather than changing their views. Framing corrections as a natural part of learning rather than a challenge to identity can help ease this resistance.

- **Confirmation Bias:** People seek out and trust information that confirms what they already believe. Encouraging them to compare different viewpoints and investigate the reliability of their sources can help mitigate this effect.

- **Social Identity and Group Loyalty:** Many people cling to misinformation because rejecting it would mean distancing themselves from their political or social group. Emphasizing that rethinking one's position can reflect intellectual strength, not disloyalty, can be effective. In the words of Adam Grant, author of *Think Again*[4],

"Changing your mind doesn't mean you've lost your integrity. It means you've evolved."

Understanding these psychological mechanisms enables us to frame conversations in ways that lower defenses rather than reinforce existing barriers.

The Role of Trust in Changing Minds

Trust plays a significant role in whether someone is open to reconsidering their beliefs. Many people distrust mainstream narratives and traditional authorities, making it difficult to persuade them using traditional sources of authority. However, personal relationships often hold more sway than abstract facts. As Ezra Klein wrote in *Why We're Polarized*[5], "In an era of fractured authority, trust is built not through credentials, but through relationships."

Building trust involves:

- **Engaging in ongoing dialogue** rather than one-off debates.

- **Demonstrating intellectual humility** by admitting when you don't have all the answers.

- **Reinforcing shared values** to create common ground.

- **Avoiding public shaming**, which can cause people to dig in rather than reconsider.

When people trust the messenger, they are more receptive to the message. This is why close friends and family members are often in the best position to influence someone's beliefs.

Conclusion

Changing minds is difficult, especially when misinformation is tied to personal identity and group loyalty. However, through empathy, patience, strategic questioning, and trust-building, it is possible to open meaningful dialogue with those trapped in misinformation.

By focusing on small cracks in belief systems—instead of attempting to overturn entire worldviews—people may become more open to self-reflection. Understanding the psychological barriers to truth can also help reduce defensiveness and encourage dialogue.

Ultimately, the goal is not to force others to adopt a particular viewpoint but to equip them with the skills necessary to evaluate claims with clarity and independence. By fostering a culture of curiosity and respectful discourse, we can begin to weaken the grip of misinformation and help restore productive political dialogue.

The final chapter will explore the role of education and fact-based discourse in preserving democracy, highlighting the systemic changes needed to prevent the spread of misinformation at a broader level.

Chapter 17

The Role of Education and Fact-Based Discourse in Saving Democracy

If misinformation is left unchecked, democracy itself is at risk[1]. The survival of democratic institutions depends on an informed electorate that can critically evaluate political claims, resist manipulation, and engage in reasoned debate. However, the decline of civic education, the rise of hyper-partisan media, and the growing influence of misinformation have severely weakened public discourse. This chapter explores the systemic changes needed to combat ignorance, including reforms in education and media, along with broader structural solutions.

The Decline of Civic Education in America

A well-functioning democracy requires citizens who understand the principles of governance, the importance of checks and balances, and the responsibilities of civic engagement. However, civic education in the United States has been in steady decline for decades[2]. Many schools provide only minimal instruction on civic principles and analytical skills, leaving young people unprepared to navigate the complexities of political life. This educational gap has serious consequences, as it allows misinformation to take root and spread more easily among an uninformed populace.

Historically, civic education was a fundamental component of American schooling, with a strong emphasis on the rights and responsibilities of citizenship. However, as standardized testing and STEM (Science, Technology, Engineering, and Mathematics) education have become a focus, civics education has been deprioritized. Today, many students graduate high school with little understanding of how government functions, the electoral process, or the historical struggles to establish and maintain democracy. This lack of foundational knowledge creates a vacuum which misinformation can fill.

Civic education is essential for developing the skills necessary for democratic participation, including:

- **Understanding the Constitution and the Bill of Rights:** Citizens must grasp the legal framework that defines their rights and limits government power.

- **Recognizing the functions and limits of government branches:** Many Americans lack basic knowledge about how laws are made, enforced, and interpreted.

- **Differentiating between credible sources of information and propaganda:** A core skill in combating misinformation is the ability to assess the reliability of information.

- **Encouraging informed voting and engagement in political processes:** Without understanding the impact of policies and elections, citizens are less likely to participate in democracy.

The decline of civic literacy has contributed to widespread political disengagement and vulnerability to misinformation. As education scholar Joel Westheimer wrote in *What Kind of Citizen?*[3], "The best defense against the politics of fear and division is a citizenry that thinks critically, is well-informed, and is engaged in the democratic process."

Without a strong foundation in democratic principles, citizens are more likely to accept misleading claims, support anti-democratic policies, or disengage from politics altogether[4]. This makes it easier for bad actors to manipulate public opinion, as many individuals lack the critical thinking skills necessary to scrutinize political narratives.

To address this crisis, schools must prioritize comprehensive civic education. This includes:

- **Integrating media literacy and critical thinking into curricula** to help students analyze news, recognize biases, and verify sources.

- **Teaching students about misinformation and cognitive biases** so they can identify manipulation tactics used in political discourse.

- **Facilitating debate and discussion** that exposes students to multiple perspectives and fosters open-mindedness.

- **Requiring civic engagement projects** that connect students with real-world democratic processes, such as attending town hall meetings, volunteering for political organizations, or participating in student government.

One of the most effective ways to counteract misinformation is to teach students *how* to think, not *what* to think. Developing a habit of questioning assumptions and weighing evidence from multiple perspectives prepares individuals to resist propaganda and ideological manipulation. This is especially crucial in an era where social media amplifies false information at an unprecedented rate.

Beyond K-12 education, civic literacy should be promoted in higher education, workplaces, and community programs. Adult education initiatives, public awareness campaigns, and online resources can help close the knowledge gap for those who did not receive strong civic instruction in school. Libraries, nonprofit organizations, and even social media platforms could serve as valuable partners in promoting civic literacy.

A renewed emphasis on civic education is critical for equipping future generations with the tools needed to preserve democracy. However, education alone is not enough. Structural reforms in media accountability are also necessary.

The Need for Structural Reforms in Media Accountability

The media plays a crucial role in shaping public perception, yet the current media landscape rewards sensationalism over accuracy[5]. The shift from traditional journalism to digital, engagement-driven news has created an ecosystem where misinformation spreads rapidly, often outpacing corrections and fact-based reporting[6].

Several factors contribute to the misinformation crisis:

- **The profit-driven nature of media companies:** Outlets prioritize sensational stories that drive clicks and engagement, often at the expense of accuracy.

- **The decline of local journalism:** Local newspapers, which historically held public officials accountable, have been decimated, leaving national outlets and social media influencers to fill the void.

- **Algorithm-driven content curation:** Social media platforms amplify polarizing content, reinforcing ideological echo chambers where misinformation thrives.

To combat these issues, structural reforms in media accountability are necessary[7].

Possible solutions include:

- **Strengthening Independent Fact-Checking Organizations**
  - Public and private funding for nonpartisan fact-checking initiatives.
  - Integration of fact-checking tools into search engines and social media platforms.
  - Greater visibility for verified corrections to counteract viral misinformation.

- **Reforming Algorithmic Incentives**
  - Social media companies should prioritize credibility over engagement.
  - Platforms should be transparent about how content is ranked and recommended.
  - Users should have the ability to customize their feeds to emphasize fact-based news over sensationalized content.

- **Holding Media Companies Accountable for Deliberate Misinformation**
  - Establishing stricter defamation laws to penalize repeated disinformation campaigns.
  - Creating industry standards for journalistic integrity, with penalties for repeated violations.
  - Encouraging news literacy initiatives that help consumers identify reliable sources.

While these reforms must be carefully balanced to protect free speech, it is clear that allowing misinformation to spread unchecked has dire consequences for democracy.

Ultimately, restoring accountability in the media requires a multi-pronged approach: improving transparency, strengthening fact-checking institutions, reforming profit-driven news algorithms, and promoting a culture of responsible journalism. In addition to media accountability, broader public trust in institutions must also be restored.

The Role of Public Institutions in Restoring Trust

Beyond education and media reform, public institutions must play a role in restoring faith in fact-based discourse. In recent years, declining trust in government, academia, and scientific institutions has made it easier for misinformation to flourish. As journalist Dan Froomkin noted in *PressThink*[8], "Trust is earned when institutions demonstrate transparency, humility, and a consistent commitment to serving the public rather than preserving their own authority."

To restore trust, institutions must take proactive steps to rebuild credibility and engage with the public in transparent, meaningful ways:

- **Government Transparency Initiatives**
  - Ensuring access to government data and decision-making processes can help counter conspiracy theories that thrive on secrecy and speculation.
  - Public records, legislative discussions, and policy deliberations should be made more accessible through digital platforms and open government initiatives.

- o Proactively addressing misinformation by releasing clear, factual information can prevent bad-faith actors from filling information gaps with misleading narratives.
- **Investment in Public Broadcasting and Nonprofit Journalism**
  - o Strengthening public broadcasting networks can provide citizens with reliable, fact-based journalism free from corporate or partisan influence.
  - o Expanding funding for nonprofit investigative journalism organizations can help counteract the financial pressures that incentivize clickbait journalism in for-profit media outlets.
  - o Encouraging grants and fellowships for long-form investigative reporting can ensure that critical issues receive in-depth analysis rather than surface-level sensationalism.
- **Improving Public Communication from Scientific Institutions**
  - o Scientific agencies and research institutions must communicate their findings more effectively to the general public, reducing the gap between experts and laypeople.
  - o Simplifying complex information into digestible formats, such as visual storytelling, podcasts, and interactive reports, can make research more accessible.
  - o Creating direct lines of communication between scientists and communities through public forums and outreach programs can foster trust and engagement.

Unfortunately, the direction being pursued by the second Trump administration is exactly opposite to the suggestions made here. Government is becoming less transparent, defunding of public broadcasting is being attempted and communications have been halted at U.S. governmental scientific institutions.

Conclusion

The fight against misinformation is not just an intellectual pursuit—it is a battle for the survival of democracy itself. Without systemic reforms in education, media accountability, and public trust, democratic institutions will continue to erode under the weight of propaganda and manipulation.

The solutions outlined in this book—from promoting critical thinking and media literacy to engaging in productive conversations and advocating for structural changes—offer a roadmap for countering ignorance and misinformation. However, these efforts require collective action. Individuals, educators, policymakers, and media organizations must all play a role in defending truth.

Breaking free from ignorance is not easy, but it is essential. A well-informed society is the foundation of a healthy democracy. By embracing education, media reform, and civic engagement, we can build a future where misinformation loses its grip, and democracy prevails.

Afterword: Theoretical No More—
Democracy Under Siege

As this book was being finalized, Donald Trump returned to the presidency. The dangers outlined in these pages are no longer theoretical. They are pursued openly—often in brazen defiance of constitutional norms and democratic principles.

Within the first 100 days of his second term, Trump signed more than 140 executive orders—surpassing the pace of any modern president[1]. These directives have targeted core democratic institutions, dismantling federal regulatory bodies and bypassing congressional oversight. The newly formed Department of Government Efficiency (DOGE), led by Elon Musk, has rapidly moved to dismantle or absorb agencies like the Department of Education, the Environmental Protection Agency, and the Consumer Financial Protection Bureau—advancing the long-standing goal of "deconstructing the administrative state[2]."

More than 1,500 individuals convicted for their role in the January 6th insurrection have been pardoned[3]. The symbolism is chilling: those who sought to overturn a democratic election are now recast as patriots. Trump has revived efforts to end birthright citizenship—despite the clear protections of the 14th Amendment[4]—and launched a sweeping deportation initiative that, legal experts warn, violates both U.S. and international law[5].

Simultaneously, the administration has moved to eliminate all diversity, equity, and inclusion (DEI) initiatives across federal agencies[6], while introducing a "patriotic education" curriculum that whitewashes American history and erases the contributions and struggles of marginalized groups[7]. These are not ordinary policy debates—they are attempts to rewrite the national narrative in service of a cult of personality.

Trump's hostility to the press has intensified. In addition to continuing his attacks on legacy media as "fake news," his administration has barred outlets like NPR, CNN, and the Associated Press from White House briefings. Independent journalists now face mounting restrictions and rising threats.

In many cases, Trump's messaging is echoed—and amplified—by a tightly aligned media ecosystem. Foremost among them is Fox News, which functions less as a watchdog than as a mouthpiece. For millions of Americans, this ecosystem constructs an alternate reality where dissent is treason, courts are corrupt, and truth is whatever the leader declares.

As Timothy Snyder warns in *On Tyranny*: "To abandon facts is to abandon freedom. If nothing is true, then no one can criticize power, because there is no basis upon which to do so."

Perhaps most alarming is the erosion of constitutional checks and balances. Trump has repeatedly challenged the authority of the judiciary[8], defied unfavorable rulings[9], and signaled his intent to reshape the court system itself[10]. Inspectors General and career civil servants have been removed or replaced by loyalists[11,12,13]. Even Congress has been sidelined. The result is a dangerous centralization of power—one that mirrors the aspirations of authoritarian regimes and mocks the safeguards envisioned by the Founders.

These developments are not aberrations. They represent the logical outcome of the disinformation strategies explored throughout this book: a propaganda machine powerful enough to override reality, a loyalist base conditioned to distrust all outside sources, and a leader unrestrained by shame, scrutiny, or precedent.

In this environment, truth now struggles to remain the foundation of public judgment and policy. It competes with lies in a contest where confusion is the goal—and clarity the casualty.

The cult-like nature of Trump's movement has never been more apparent. Loyalty to Trump has replaced loyalty to law, country, and democratic principles. Veteran Republicans who question him are denounced. Policy is shaped less by evidence than by performance. Projection remains a signature tactic: Trump accuses others of the very abuses he commits. As Hannah Arendt once observed[14], "The ideal subject of totalitarian rule is not the convinced Nazi or the convinced Communist, but people for whom the distinction between fact and fiction ... no longer exists."

And yet, large portions of the public remain unaware—or unconcerned. Many Americans, insulated by ideological media bubbles, rarely encounter accurate reporting. Project 2025, though being implemented in plain sight, is still dismissed by many as a hoax or liberal exaggeration. The media landscape has fractured so deeply that tens of millions of citizens are now cut off from a shared understanding of reality.

Unfortunately, near-term improvements are unlikely. Structural media reform is improbable in a deregulated, profit-driven information ecosystem. Critical thinking takes years to cultivate—and is actively undermined in many schools and communities. Meanwhile, social media platforms, largely unmoderated, continue to accelerate the spread of falsehoods. The very conditions that enabled widespread political ignorance not only persist but are, in some cases, deliberately reinforced.

President Barack Obama put it simply in 2022[15]: "If we don't have the capacity to distinguish what's true from what's false, then by definition the marketplace of ideas doesn't work. And by definition, our democracy doesn't work."

Still, there is hope. Grassroots efforts to promote truth, expand civic education, and rebuild trust in public institutions may be slow, but they are essential. Every citizen who challenges disinformation, supports independent journalism, or teaches children to evaluate evidence strengthens democracy.

The weaponization of ignorance threatens not only American democracy but global stability. In 2025, the Bulletin of the Atomic Scientists reset the Doomsday Clock to its most dire setting on record. In its warning[16], the organization stated:

"The dangers we have just listed are greatly exacerbated by a potent threat multiplier: the spread of misinformation, disinformation, and conspiracy theories that degrade the communication ecosystem and increasingly blur the line between truth and falsehood. Advances in AI are making it easier to spread false or inauthentic information across the Internet—and harder to detect it. At the same time, nations are engaging in cross-border efforts to use disinformation and other forms of propaganda to subvert elections, while some technology, media, and political leaders aid the spread of lies and conspiracy theories. This corruption of the information ecosystem undermines the public discourse and honest debate upon which democracy depends... The battered information landscape is also producing leaders who discount science and endeavor to suppress free speech and human rights, compromising the fact-based public discussions that are required to combat the enormous threats facing the world."

Originally, I set out to understand why so many people—especially intelligent people—believe lies. That question led to a broader investigation: how disinformation operates, how ignorance is cultivated, and how even truth becomes powerless in a climate shaped by tribalism, fear, and manipulation.

But the project became something more. What began as a personal exploration has become a mission in defense of truth and democracy.

Democracy is not self-sustaining. It demands an informed electorate, a functioning public sphere, and a shared commitment to truth. I hope the ideas in this book inspire you, as they inspired me, to seek the truth, defend it fiercely, and never surrender it to those who would bury it in lies.

Ultimately, our collective willingness to confront weaponized ignorance will determine whether American democracy is diminished by its enemies—or renewed by its defenders. As the nation approaches its 250th birthday, the responsibility lies with all of us to ensure that truth, reason, and democracy not only survive—but thrive.

Acknowledgements

I wish to thank my parents for instilling in me a commitment to humanistic values—an early sense of justice, empathy, and a willingness to fight for what I believe in.

Thank you to the many friends and colleagues who read the manuscript and offered suggestions. I may not have incorporated every piece of advice, but I deeply appreciate all the feedback I received.

Finally, a heartfelt thank you to my wife, who has supported me in my various endeavors—and who, thankfully, still shares the same ethical, moral, and political views after more than 50 years of marriage.

Glossary of Terms

Alternative Facts—A term popularized to describe demonstrably false statements presented as truth, often to mislead or manipulate public perception.

Apocalyptic Thinking—A mindset that perceives political or social events as leading to catastrophic or end-of-the-world scenarios, often used to manipulate fear and urgency.

Availability Heuristic—A cognitive bias where people overestimate the importance of information that comes readily to mind, often leading to distorted perceptions of reality.

Authoritarian Leadership—A style of governance where power is concentrated in a leader or small elite, often at the expense of democratic norms and individual freedoms.

Backfire Effect—A psychological phenomenon where exposure to contradictory information reinforces existing beliefs rather than changing them.

Bias—A tendency to favor one perspective, ideology, or outcome over others, often at the expense of objectivity.

Binary Worldview—A perspective that simplifies complex issues into two opposing sides, often ignoring nuance and fostering polarization.

Black-and-White Thinking—A cognitive distortion where individuals see issues in extremes, failing to recognize middle ground or complexity.

Cognitive Dissonance—The psychological discomfort experienced when holding conflicting beliefs or encountering information that challenges one's worldview.

Confirmation Bias—The tendency to seek out, interpret, and remember information that supports preexisting beliefs while ignoring contradictory evidence.

Conspiracy Theory—A belief that significant events or outcomes are secretly controlled by powerful groups, often without credible evidence.

Critical Thinking—The ability to objectively analyze and evaluate information, arguments, and claims to form reasoned judgments.

Culture War—The ideological and social conflicts between groups with opposing values, particularly in politics, religion, and social issues.

Cultural Anxieties—The fears and uncertainties experienced by groups regarding societal change, often exploited for political gain.

Cultural Displacement—The perception that one's cultural identity is being threatened or replaced by outside influences.

Deep State—A term used to suggest that unelected government officials and elites secretly control policy decisions, often with conspiratorial undertones.

Disinformation—False or misleading information intentionally spread to deceive and manipulate public opinion; a subset of misinformation

Dunning-Kruger Effect—A cognitive bias where individuals with low expertise overestimate their knowledge and competence.

Echo Chamber—A situation where individuals are exposed only to information and opinions that reinforce their existing views, limiting diverse perspectives.

Fear-Mongering—The use of fear to influence public opinion and manipulate behavior, often by exaggerating threats or dangers.

Fake News—Fabricated or misleading news stories designed to deceive readers, often spread through social media or partisan outlets.

Filter Bubbles—Digital environments where individuals are exposed only to content that aligns with their existing beliefs, limiting exposure to diverse perspectives.

Gaslighting—A form of psychological manipulation where a person or group deliberately causes someone to doubt their own perception of reality.

Grievance Politics—The exploitation of perceived injustices or victimhood for political gain, often to mobilize supporters against an opposing group.

Group Loyalty—The tendency to prioritize the interests and beliefs of one's group over external perspectives or objective truth.

Groupthink—A psychological phenomenon where the desire for conformity within a group suppresses dissenting opinions and critical thinking.

Ideological Polarization—The increasing division between political or social groups, often leading to hostility and reduced willingness to compromise.

Ignorance—A lack of knowledge, awareness, or understanding, which can be natural, willful, or manipulated by external influences.

Identity-Based Loyalty—Political or ideological allegiance driven primarily by personal or group identity rather than policy or evidence.

Illusory Truth Effect—The tendency to believe false information as true after repeated exposure.

In-Group Bias—A preference for members of one's own group over outsiders, often leading to discrimination and exclusion.

Intellectual Humility—The recognition of the limits of one's knowledge and a willingness to consider alternative perspectives.

Local Journalism—News organizations that focus on community-based reporting, often essential for an informed electorate but increasingly underfunded.

MAGA—Short for "Make America Great Again," a slogan associated with Donald Trump's political movement, often used to describe its supporters and ideology.

Mainstream Media (MSM)—Large, established news organizations often accused of bias by both ends of the political spectrum.

Manipulative Rhetoric—Language crafted to emotionally manipulate or deceive an audience for political or ideological gain.

Media Fragmentation & Social Reinforcement—The division of media consumption into specialized outlets that reinforce existing beliefs rather than challenge them.

Media Literacy—The ability to critically analyze and evaluate media messages to distinguish fact from misinformation.

Misinformation—False or misleading information. It may be spread unintentionally; or deliberately in the case of disinformation.

Motivated Reasoning—The tendency to interpret information in a way that confirms preexisting beliefs or desires, rather than objectively evaluating evidence.

Narrative Control—The strategic shaping of public perception by controlling the information available through media, political messaging, and censorship.

News Deserts—Communities with little to no access to local journalism, increasing reliance on national media and social networks for information.

Partisan Media—News organizations or commentators that cater to a specific political ideology, often at the expense of objectivity.

Partisan—Strong allegiance to a political party, often leading to biased perspectives and resistance to opposing viewpoints.

Personality-Driven Politics—A political landscape where charisma and individual personas overshadow policy discussions and substantive governance.

Political Manipulation—The strategic use of misinformation, emotional appeals, and psychological tactics to control public perception and behavior.

Political Tribalism—A form of group identity where loyalty to a political ideology or party overrides objectivity and reason.

Post-Truth—A cultural and political condition where emotional appeals and personal beliefs hold more influence over public opinion than objective facts.

Propaganda—Biased or misleading information used to promote a political cause or agenda, often employing emotional appeals and selective facts.

Scandal Fatigue—The public's desensitization to political or media scandals due to their frequent occurrence.

Skepticism—The practice of questioning claims and seeking evidence before forming beliefs.

Social Identity—A person's sense of self as it relates to their membership in social, political, or cultural groups.

Strategic Deception—The deliberate use of misleading information to manipulate public perception or achieve political goals.

Strategic Misinformation—The calculated spread of false information to mislead opponents or manipulate public perception.

Strongman Appeal—The admiration of authoritarian figures who promise simple, decisive solutions to complex problems.

Thought-Terminating Clichés—Simplistic phrases used to dismiss critical thinking and shut down debate.

Tribal Epistemology—A concept where truth is determined by group loyalty rather than objective evidence or reasoned argument.

Truth Decay—The diminishing role of objective facts in shaping public opinion, leading to increased reliance on personal beliefs and misinformation.

This Glossary provides concise definitions of key terms used throughout *Weaponization of Ignorance*. These definitions aim to clarify complex concepts and ensure consistency in discussions throughout the book.

Chapter References

Chapter 1: The Cognitive Roots of Misinformation

1. Kahneman, D. (2011). *Thinking, fast and slow*. Farrar, Straus and Giroux.

2. Somin, I. (2016). Democracy and political ignorance: Why smaller government is smarter (2nd ed.). Stanford University Press.

3. Lodge, M., & Taber, C. S. (2006). "Motivated skepticism in the evaluation of political beliefs." *American Journal of Political Science*, 50(3), 755–769. doi:10.1111/j.1540-5907.2006.00214.x

4. Kunda, Z. (1990). "The case for motivated reasoning." *Psychological Bulletin*, 108(3), 480–498. doi:10.1037/0033-2909.108.3.480

5. Nyhan, B., & Reifler, J. (2010). "When corrections fail: The persistence of political misperceptions." *Political Behavior*, 32(2), 303–330.

6. Mason, L. (2018). *Uncivil agreement: How politics became our identity*. University of Chicago Press.

7. Festinger, L. (1957). *A theory of cognitive dissonance*. Stanford University Press.

8. Dunning, D. (2011). "The Dunning–Kruger effect: On being ignorant of one's own ignorance." *Advances in Experimental Social Psychology*, 44, 247–296. doi:10.1016/B978-0-12-385522-0.00005-6

9. Rozenblit, L., & Keil, F. C. (2002). "The misunderstood limits of folk science: An illusion of explanatory depth." *Cognitive Science*, 26(5), 521–562. doi:10.1207/s15516709cog2605_1

10. Fisher, M., Goddu, M. K., & Keil, F. C. (2015). "Searching for explanations: How the internet inflates estimates of internal knowledge." *Journal of Experimental Psychology: General*, 144(3), 674–687.

11. Tversky, A., & Kahneman, D. (1973). "Availability: A heuristic for judging frequency and probability." *Cognitive Psychology*, 5(2), 207–232. doi:10.1016/0010-0285(73)90033-9

12. Sunstein, C. R. (2001). *Republic: Divided democracy in the age of social media*. Princeton University Press.

13. Martel, C., Pennycook, G., & Rand, D. G. (2020). "Reliance on emotion promotes belief in fake news." *Cognitive Research: Principles and Implications*, 5(47).

14. Porter, T., & Schumann, K. (2018). "Intellectual humility and openness to opposing views." *Self and Identity*, 17(2), 139–162.

15. Basol, M., Roozenbeek, J., & van der Linden, S. (2024). "Media literacy interventions improve resilience to misinformation: A meta-analysis." *Communication Research*.

16. Fazio, L. K., & Pennycook, G. (2024). "Critical thinking predicts reduced susceptibility to misinformation across the ideological spectrum." *PNAS Nexus*, 3(10), pgae361.

17. Marius, D., & Popescu, R. (2024). "Media literacy and critical thinking as tools for combating disinformation." *Journal of Media and Social Influence*.

18. Lee, A., & Castillo, M. (2023). "Critical thinking and media literacy in an age of misinformation." *Journal of Education and Information Literacy*, 12(2).

19. van der Linden, S. (2023). *Foolproof: Why we fall for misinformation and how to build immunity*. W. W. Norton & Company.

Chapter 2: The Role of Misinformation in Shaping Beliefs

1. Fazio, L. K., Brashier, N. M., Payne, B. K., & Marsh, E. J. (2015). "Knowledge does not protect against illusory truth." *Journal of Experimental Psychology: General, 144*(5), 993–1002.

2. Martel, C., Pennycook, G., & Rand, D. G. (2020). "Reliance on emotion promotes belief in fake news." *Cognitive Research: Principles and Implications, 5*(47).

3. Benkler, Y., Faris, R., & Roberts, H. (2018). *Network propaganda: Manipulation, disinformation, and radicalization in American politics*. Oxford University Press.

4. Flaxman, S., Goel, S., & Rao, J. M. (2016). "Filter bubbles, echo chambers, and online news consumption." *Public Opinion Quarterly, 80*(S1), 298–320.

5. Ball, P., & Maxmen, A. (2020). "The epic battle against coronavirus misinformation." *Nature, 580*(7803), 371–374.

6. Kunda, Z. (1990). "The case for motivated reasoning." *Psychological Bulletin, 108*(3), 480–498.

7. Nyhan, B., & Reifler, J. (2010). "When corrections fail: The persistence of political misperceptions." *Political Behavior, 32*(2), 303–330.

8. **8.** Pew Research Center. (2024, November 18). *America's news influencers*. Retrieved from: www.pewresearch.org/journalism/2024/11/18/americas-news-influencers

9. Bakshy, E., Messing, S., & Adamic, L. A. (2015). "Exposure to ideologically diverse news and opinion on Facebook." *Science, 348*(6239), 1130–1132.

10. Muirhead, R., & Rosenblum, N. L. (2019). *A lot of people are saying: The new conspiracism and the assault on democracy*. Princeton University Press.

11. Smith, D. (2025, March 23). "Trump's defiance of court orders is 'testing the fences' of the rule of law." *The Guardian*.

12. Desikan, A. (2020, September 15). "Political officials undermine CDC scientists' COVID-19 studies." *Union of Concerned Scientists*. Retrieved from blog.ucs.org/anita-desikan/political-officials-undermine-covid-19-studies

13. Simmons-Duffin, S. (2020, September 25). "Emails reveal how Trump appointees pressured CDC to alter COVID reports." *NPR*.

14. Goldberg, M. (2021, June 14). "Critical race panic is fueling a new moral panic." *The New York Times*.

15. Qiu, L. (2018, October 22). "How Trump's caravan of migrants became a GOP campaign strategy." *The New York Times*.

Chapter 3: Media Bubbles and Echo Chambers

1. Hindman, M. (2009). *The myth of digital democracy*. Princeton University Press.

2. History.com Editors. (2020). "CNN launches first 24-hour news network." *History.com*.

3. Wikipedia contributors. (2024). "History of CNN." *Wikipedia: The Free Encyclopedia*.

4. Levendusky, M. S. (2013). *How partisan media polarize America*. University of Chicago Press.

5. Tufekci, Z. (2017). *Twitter and tear gas: The power and fragility of networked protest*. Yale University Press.

6. Garrett, R. K. (2009). "Echo chambers online? Politically motivated selective exposure among internet news users." *Journal of Computer-Mediated Communication, 14*(2), 265–285.

7. Ball, M. (2022). "The OANN effect: How fringe news networks push Fox further right." *Columbia Journalism Review.*

8. Jamieson, K. H., & Cappella, J. N. (2008). *Echo chamber: Rush Limbaugh and the conservative media establishment.* Oxford University Press.

9. Gladstone, B. (2017). *The trouble with reality: A rumination on moral panic in our time.* Workman Publishing.

10. Haidt, J. (2012). *The righteous mind: Why good people are divided by politics and religion.* Vintage.

11. Rosenwald, M. (2021). *Hostile takeover: How conservative media reshaped America.* W. W. Norton & Company.

12. Barberá, P. (2015). "Social media, echo chambers, and political polarization." *SSRN Working Paper.*

13. Wardle, C., & Derakhshan, H. (2017). *Information disorder: Toward an interdisciplinary framework for research and policy making.* Council of Europe.

14. Vosoughi, S., Roy, D., & Aral, S. (2018). "The spread of true and false news online." *Science, 359*(6380), 1146–1151.

15. Postman, N. (1985). *Amusing ourselves to death: Public discourse in the age of show business.* Viking Penguin.

16. Ribeiro, M. H., Ottoni, R., West, R., Almeida, V. A. F., & Meira Jr, W. (2020). "Auditing radicalization pathways on YouTube." *Proceedings of the ACM Conference on Fairness, Accountability, and Transparency (FAccT).*

17. Tufekci, Z. (2018, March 10). "YouTube, the great radicalizer." *The New York Times.*

18. Abernathy, P. M. (2020). *News deserts and ghost newspapers: Will local news survive?* University of North Carolina Press.

19. Nyhan, B., & Reifler, J. (2010). "When corrections fail: The persistence of political misperceptions." *Political Behavior, 32*(2), 303–330.

20. McChesney, R. W. (2010). *The death and life of American journalism: The media revolution that will begin the world again.* Nation Books.

21. Ripley, A. (2018, July). "Complicating the narratives." *The Atlantic.*

Chapter 4: The Psychology of Conspiracy Theories

1. van Prooijen, J. W. (2022). *The psychology of conspiracy theories.* Routledge.

2. Martel, C., Pennycook, G., & Rand, D. G. (2020). "Reliance on emotion promotes belief in fake news." *Cognitive Research: Principles and Implications, 5*(47). doi:10.1186/s41235-020-00252-3

3. Uscinski, J. E. (2020). *Conspiracy theories: A primer.* Rowman & Littlefield.

4. Olmsted, K. S. (2009). *Real enemies: Conspiracy theories and American democracy, World War I to 9/11.* Oxford University Press.

5. Lifton, R. J. (1961). *Thought reform and the psychology of totalism: A study of 'brainwashing' in China.* University of North Carolina Press.

6. McIntyre, L. (2018). *Post-truth.* MIT Press.

7. Swisher, K. (2023). *Under the influence: The tech industry and the end of truth.* Simon & Schuster.

8. Douglas, K. M., Sutton, R. M., & Cichocka, A. (2017). "The psychology of conspiracy theories." *Current Directions in Psychological Science, 26*(6), 538–542.

9. Applebaum, A. (2020). *Twilight of democracy: The seductive lure of authoritarianism.* Doubleday.

10. Business Insider. (2021). "QAnon conspiracy theory, misinformation fueled Capitol riots."

11. Harwell, D., Stanley-Becker, I., Nakhlawi, R., & Timberg, C. (2021). "QAnon reshaped Trump's party and radicalized believers. The Capitol siege may just be the start." *The Washington Post.*

12. Zadrozny, B., & Collins, B. (2021, January 7). "How the 'Stop the Steal' movement outlived Trump." *NBC News.*

13. Vosoughi, S., Roy, D., & Aral, S. (2018). "The spread of true and false news online." *Science, 359*(6380), 1146–1151.

14. Wallace, J., Goldsmith-Pinkham, P., & Schwartz, J. L. (2023). "Excess death rates for Republican and Democratic registered voters in Florida and Ohio during the COVID-19 pandemic." *JAMA Internal Medicine, 183*(9), 1023–1030.

15. Lewandowsky, S., Ecker, U. K. H., & Cook, J. (2017). "Beyond misinformation: Understanding and coping with the 'post-truth' era." *Journal of Applied Research in Memory and Cognition, 6*(4), 353–369.

16. LaFrance, A. (2020). "The prophecies of Q." *The Atlantic.*

17. Benkler, Y., Faris, R., & Roberts, H. (2018). *Network propaganda: Manipulation, disinformation, and radicalization in American politics.* Oxford University Press.

18. Granados Samayoa, J., & Albarracín, D. (2024). "Bypassing as a non-confrontational influence strategy." *Current Opinion in Psychology, 54*, 101–106.

19. Mihailidis, P., & Viotty, S. (2017). "Spreadable spectacle in digital culture: Civic expression, fake news, and the role of media literacies in 'post-fact' society." *American Behavioral Scientist, 61*(4), 441–454.

20. Nyhan, B., & Reifler, J. (2010). "When corrections fail: The persistence of political misperceptions." *Political Behavior, 32*(2), 303–330.

21. Freedom House. (2024). *Freedom in the world 2024: The mounting damage of democratic decline.*

Chapter 5: The Dangers of Blind Tribalism and Cult-Like Behavior

1. Muirhead, R., & Rosenblum, N. L. (2019). A Lot of People Are Saying: The New Conspiracism and the Assault on Democracy. Princeton University Press.

2. Mason, L. (2018). Uncivil Agreement: How Politics Became Our Identity. University of Chicago Press.

3. Tajfel, H., & Turner, J. C. (1979) "An Integrative Theory of Intergroup Conflict." In W. G. Austin & S. Worchel (eds.), The Social Psychology of Intergroup Relations, pp. 33–47. Brooks/Cole.

4. Festinger, L. (1957). A Theory of Cognitive Dissonance. Stanford University Press.

5. Lakoff, G. (2009).The Political Mind: A Cognitive Scientist's Guide to Your Brain and Its Politics. Penguin Books.

6. Ghaffary, S. (Oct. 30, 2020). "Trump's Personality Cult Plays a Part in His Political Appeal." Scientific American.

7. Hassan, S. (2020). The Cult of Trump: A Leading Cult Expert Explains How the President Uses Mind Control. Free Press.

8. Lifton, R. J. (1961). Thought Reform and the Psychology of Totalism: A Study of "Brainwashing" in China. University of North Carolina Press.

9. Levitsky, S., & Ziblatt, D. (2018). How Democracies Die. Crown Publishing.

10. Martel, C., Pennycook, G., & Rand, D. G. (2020). "Reliance on Emotion Promotes Belief in Fake News." Cognitive Research: Principles and Implications, vol. 5, no. 1, p. 47.

11. Coppins, M. (January 2022). "The Republican Party Is Now in Its End Stages." The Atlantic.

12. Gorski, P. S. "Trumpism: Why It Captures the Republican Base." Sociology Compass, vol. 17, no. 4, 2023, e12991.

Chapter 6: Not All Believers: Understanding the Republican Voter Base

1. Associated Press–NORC Center for Public Affairs Research. (2021, July 23). *Poll: 66% of Republicans say Biden wasn't legitimately elected.*

2. Brennan, J. (2011). *The ethics of voting.* Princeton University Press.

3. Stelter, B. (2020). *Hoax: Donald Trump, Fox News, and the dangerous distortion of truth.* Atria/One Signal Publishers.

4. Pew Research Center. (2020, September 30). *Behind Biden's 2020 rise: Black voters and suburban women.*

5. Klein, E. (2020). *Why we're polarized.* Avid Reader Press / Simon & Schuster.

6. Kahan, D. M. (2010). "Cultural cognition of scientific consensus." *Journal of Risk Research, 14*(2), 147–174.

7. Pew Research Center. (2022, October 13). *Americans' trust in government remains low.*

8. Fiske, S. T., & Taylor, S. E. (2017). *Social cognition: From brains to culture* (3rd ed.). Sage.

9. Biko, S. (2002). *I write what I like: Selected writings.* University of Chicago Press.

10. Mason, L. (2018). *Uncivil agreement: How politics became our identity*. University of Chicago Press.

11. Wiesel, E. (1999, April 12). *The perils of indifference*. Speech at the White House Millennium Lecture Series.

12. Hassan, S. (2020). *The cult of Trump: A leading cult expert explains how the president uses mind control*. Free Press.

13. Snyder, T. (2017). *On tyranny: Twenty lessons from the twentieth century*. Tim Duggan Books.

Chapter 7: Seeds of Distrust: Historical Grievances

1. Obama, B. H. (2008, April 6). *Remarks at private fundraiser in San Francisco*. Quoted in *The Guardian*, April 13, 2008.

2. Reagan, R. (1986, August 12). *Remarks to Future Farmers of America*. U.S. National Archives.

3. Limbaugh, R. (2002). *The Limbaugh Letter*, November issue. Premiere Radio Networks.

4. Nixon, R. M. (1969, November 3). *Address to the nation on the war in Vietnam*. The American Presidency Project.

5. Reagan, R. (1980, August 25). *Remarks at the Republican National Convention*. Ronald Reagan Presidential Library.

6. Troy, G. (2005). *Morning in America: How Ronald Reagan invented the 1980s*. Princeton University Press.

7. Levin, J. (2013, December 19). "The welfare queen." *Slate*.

8. Gingrich, N. (1994). *To renew America*. HarperCollins.

9. Bannon, S. (quoted in Faris, R., Roberts, H., & Zuckerman, E. [2020]). *Network propaganda: Manipulation, disinformation, and radicalization in American politics*. Oxford University Press.

10. Trump, D. J. (2017, February 17). Twitter post: www.twitter.com/realDonaldTrump/status/8327 08293516632065

11. Baldwin, J. (1963). *The fire next time*. Dial Press.

Chapter 8: Faith, Fear, and Fox: The Moral Framework of Conservative America

1. Gallup. (July 12, 2023). "Confidence in Institutions." *Gallup*.

2. Haidt, J. (2012). *The Righteous Mind: Why Good People Are Divided by Politics and Religion*. Pantheon Books

3. Lakoff, G. (2004). *Don't Think of an Elephant! Know Your Values and Frame the Debate*. Chelsea Green.

4. Jones, R. P. (2023). *The Hidden Roots of White Supremacy and the Path to a Shared American Future*. Simon & Schuster.

5. Du Mez, K. K. (2020). *Jesus and John Wayne: How White Evangelicals Corrupted a Faith and Fractured a Nation*. Liveright.

6. Hibbing, J. R., Smith, K. B., & Alford, J. R. (2013). *Predisposed: Liberals, Conservatives, and the Biology of Political Differences*. Routledge.

7. Ripley, (2021). A. *High Conflict: Why We Get Trapped and How We Get Out*. Simon & Schuster.

8. Carlson, T. (Apr. 6, 2021). "Tucker Carlson Tonight." *Fox News*.

9. Postman, N. (1985). *Amusing Ourselves to Death: Public Discourse in the Age of Show Business*. Viking.

10. Arendt, H. (1951). *The Origins of Totalitarianism*. Harcourt.

11. Lee, B. X. (ed.). (2017). *The Dangerous Case of Donald Trump: 27 Psychiatrists and Mental Health Experts Assess a President*. Thomas Dunne Books.

Chapter 9: Why Do People Believe Trump?

1. Pennycook, G., & Rand, D. G. (2018). "The implied truth effect: Attaching warnings to a subset of fake news stories increases perceived accuracy of stories without warnings." *Management Science, 66*(11), 4944–4957.

2. Levitsky, S., & Ziblatt, D. (2018). *How democracies die.* Crown Publishing Group.

3. Mercieca, J. (2020). *Demagogue for president: The rhetorical genius of Donald Trump.* Texas A&M University Press.

4. Mounk, Y. (2018). *The people vs. democracy: Why our freedom is in danger and how to save it.* Harvard University Press.

5. Stenner, K. (2005). *The authoritarian dynamic.* Cambridge University Press.

6. Burnett, M. (Creator), & Trump, D. (Host). (2004–2017). *The Apprentice* [TV series]. NBC.

7. Barstow, D., Craig, S., & Buettner, R. (2018, October 2). "Trump engaged in suspect tax schemes as he reaped riches from his father." *The New York Times.*

8. Hochschild, A. R. (2016). *Strangers in their own land: Anger and mourning on the American right.* The New Press.

9. Stanley, J. (2018). *How fascism works: The politics of us and them.* Random House.

10. Alberta, T. (2019). *American carnage: On the front lines of the Republican civil war and the rise of President Trump.* Harper.

11. Feldman, S. (2003). "Enforcing social conformity: A theory of authoritarianism." *Political Psychology, 24*(1), 41–74.

12. Applebaum, A. (2020). *Twilight of democracy: The seductive lure of authoritarianism.* Doubleday.

13. Fisher, M. (2023, September 5). "Polarization, democracy, and political violence in the United States:

What research says." *Carnegie Endowment for International Peace.*

14. Qiu, L. (2018, October 22). "How Trump's caravan of migrants became a GOP campaign strategy." *The New Yorker.*

15. Eatwell, R. (2017). *National populism: The revolt against liberal democracy.* Pelican.

16. Tajfel, H., & Turner, J. C. (1979). "An integrative theory of intergroup conflict." In W. G. Austin & S. Worchel (Eds.), *The social psychology of intergroup relations* (pp. 33–47). Brooks/Cole.

17. Mason, L. (2018). *Uncivil agreement: How politics became our identity.* University of Chicago Press.

18. Van Bavel, J. J., & Packer, D. J. (2021). "The role of identity leadership on January 6th." *Substack.*

19. Fahrenthold, D. A. (2016, October 7). "Trump recorded having extremely lewd conversation about women in 2005." *The Washington Post.*

20. Hassan, S. (2020). *The cult of Trump: A leading cult expert explains how the president uses mind control.* Free Press.

21. Dowd, M. (1998, February 22). "The price of scandal fatigue." *The New York Times.*

22. Sloan, J. W. (1998, October 21). "Suffering scandal fatigue." *Los Angeles Times.*

23. Kumlin, S., & Esaiasson, P. (2012). "Scandal fatigue? Scandal elections and satisfaction with democracy in Western Europe, 1977–2007." *British Journal of Political Science, 42*(2), 263–282.

24. Snyder, T. (2017). *On tyranny: Twenty lessons from the twentieth century.* Tim Duggan Books.

Chapter 10: The Media's Role in Shaping Political Ignorance

1. Kovach, B., & Rosenstiel, T. (2014). *The Elements of Journalism: What Newspeople Should Know and the Public Should Expect.* Crown Publishing.

2. Pariser, E. (2011). *The Filter Bubble: How the New Personalized Web Is Changing What We Read and How We Think.* Penguin Books.

3. DellaVigna, S., & Kaplan, E. (2007). "The Fox News Effect: Media Bias and Voting." *Quarterly Journal of Economics*, vol. 122, no. 3, pp. 1187–1234. https://doi.org/10.1162/qjec.122.3.1187

4. Martin, G. J., & Yurukoglu, A. (2017). "Bias in Cable News: Persuasion and Polarization." *American Economic Review*, vol. 107, no. 9, pp. 2565–2599.

5. Ball, P., & Maxmen, A. (2020). "The Epic Battle Against Coronavirus Misinformation." *Nature*, vol. 580, no. 7803, pp. 371–374.

6. Kull, S., Ramsay, C., & Lewis, E. (2010). *Misinformation and the 2010 Election: A Study of the US Electorate.* Program on International Policy Attitudes (PIPA), University of Maryland.

7. Stelter, B. (2023). *Network of Lies: The Epic Saga of Fox News, Donald Trump, and the Battle for American Democracy.* Atria/One Signal Publishers.

8. Jamieson, K. H., & Cappella, J. N. (2008). *Echo Chamber: Rush Limbaugh and the Conservative Media Establishment.* Oxford University Press.

9. Pew Research Center. (2014). *Political Polarization & Media Habits.* https://www.pewresearch.org/journalism/2014/10/21/political-polarization-media-habits

10. Benkler, Y., Faris, R., & Roberts, H. (2018). *Network Propaganda: Manipulation, Disinformation, and Radicalization in American Politics*. Oxford University Press.

11. Tufekci, Z. (2017). *Twitter and Tear Gas: The Power and Fragility of Networked Protest*. Yale University Press.

12. Vaidhyanathan, S. (2018). *Antisocial Media: How Facebook Disconnects Us and Undermines Democracy*. Oxford University Press.

13. Ribeiro, M. H., Ottoni, R., West, R., Almeida, V. A. F., & Meira, W. Jr. (2020). "Auditing Radicalization Pathways on YouTube." In *Proceedings of the 2020 Conference on Fairness, Accountability, and Transparency*, 2020, pp. 131–141. https://doi.org/10.1145/3351095.3372879

14. Lewandowsky, S., Ecker, U. K. H., & Cook, J. (2017). "Beyond Misinformation: Understanding and Coping with the 'Post-Truth' Era." *Journal of Applied Research in Memory and Cognition*, vol. 6, no. 4, pp. 353–369. https://doi.org/10.1016/j.jarmac.2017.07.008

15. Sunstein, C. R. (2001). *Republic: Divided Democracy in the Age of Social Media*. Princeton University Press.

16. Gladstone, B. (2017). *The Trouble with Reality: A Rumination on Moral Panic in Our Time*. Workman Publishing.

17. Feldman, L. (2011). "Partisan Selective Exposure and the Information Environment." *Public Opinion Quarterly*, vol. 75, no. 3, pp. 399–424. https://doi.org/10.1093/poq/nfr006

18. Gallup. (n.d.) *Trust in Mass Media Polling*. https://news.gallup.com/poll/243665/americans-trust-mass-media-edges-down.aspx

19. Vosoughi, S., Roy, D., & Aral, S. (2018). "The Spread of True and False News Online." *Science*, vol. 359, no. 6380, pp. 1146–1151. https://doi.org/10.1126/science.aap9559

Chapter 11: The Role of Fox and Partisan Media

1. Hemmer, N. (2016). *Messengers of the Right: Conservative Media and the Transformation of American Politics*. University of Pennsylvania Press.

2. Benkler, Y., Faris, R., & Roberts, H. (2018). *Network Propaganda: Manipulation, Disinformation, and Radicalization in American Politics*. Oxford University Press.

3. Taibbi, M. (2019). *Hate Inc.: Why Today's Media Makes Us Despise One Another*. OR Books.

4. Feldman, L. (2020). *The Enemy of the People: The Myths & Reality of Fake News*. Brookings Institution Press.

5. Ball, M. (2022). "The OANN Effect: How Fringe News Networks Push Fox Further Right." *Columbia Journalism Review*. https://www.cjr.org/special_report/oann-effect-fox-news.php

6. Stelter, B. (2023). *Network of Lies: The Epic Saga of Fox News, Donald Trump, and the Battle for American Democracy*. Atria/One Signal Publishers.

7. Rosenwald, M. (2021). *Hostile Takeover: How Conservative Media Reshaped America*. W. W. Norton & Company.

8. Confessore, N., Yourish, K., Buchanan, L., Byrd, A., & Cai, W. (Apr. 30, 2022). "Inside the Apocalyptic Worldview of 'Tucker Carlson Tonight'." *The New York Times*.

9. Stelter, B. (2020). *Hoax: Donald Trump, Fox News, and the Dangerous Distortion of Truth*. One Signal Publishers.

10. Jamieson, K. H., & Cappella, J. N. (2008). *Echo Chamber: Rush Limbaugh and the Conservative Media Establishment*. Oxford University Press.

11. Sullivan, M. (2020). *Ghosting the News: Local Journalism and the Crisis of American Democracy*. Columbia Global Reports.

12. Rauch, J. (2021). *The Constitution of Knowledge: A Defense of Truth*. Brookings Institution Press.

Chapter 12: How Political Figures Manipulate their Base

1. Nichols, T. (2017). *The Death of Expertise: The Campaign Against Established Knowledge and Why It Matters*. Oxford University Press.

2. Center for American Progress. (Apr. 15, 2025). *100 Days of the Trump Administration's Foreign Policy: Global Chaos, American Weakness, and Human Suffering*. https://www.americanprogress.org

3. Coppins, M. (2022). "The Republican Party Is Now in Its End Stages." *The Atlantic*. https://www.theatlantic.com/magazine/archive/2022/01/republican-party-collapse-trump/620843

4. Corn, D. (2022). *American Psychosis: A Historical Investigation of How the Republican Party Went Crazy*. Twelve.

5. Stanley, J. (2018). *How Fascism Works: The Politics of Us and Them*. Random House.

6. Pleat, Z. (Oct. 25, 2022). "Mainstream Media Coverage of Crime Pushes Right-Wing Narratives That Blame Democrats, but Crime Is Worse in GOP-Controlled Areas." *Media Matters for America*.

7. Karefa-Johnson, R. (Nov. 8, 2022). "Stories About Crime Are Rife with Misinformation and Racism, Critics Say." *NPR*.

8. Pew Research Center. (Oct. 31, 2022). *Violent Crime Is a Key Midterm Voting Issue, but What Does the Data Say?*

9. Gold, M., & Huynh, A. (Apr. 2, 2024). "Trump Again Invokes 'Blood Bath' and Dehumanizes Migrants in Border Remarks." *The New York Times*.

10. Pomerantsev, P. (2019). *This Is Not Propaganda: Adventures in the War Against Reality*. PublicAffairs.

11. Young, C. (2024). *Wrong: How Media, Politics, and Identity Drive Our Appetite for Misinformation*. Prometheus Books.

12. McQuade, B. (2024). *Attack from Within: How Disinformation Is Sabotaging America*. St. Martin's Press.

13. Levitsky, S., & Ziblatt, D. (2018). *How Democracies Die*. Crown Publishing.

14. Gerson, M. (Nov. 17, 2011). "How Republican Conformity Is Ruining Politics." *The Washington Post*.

15. Brookings Institution. (2023). *Rebuilding Trust in Democracy: A Policy Roadmap*.

Chapter 13: The Echo Chamber of Republican Leadership

1. Brock, D. (2004). *The Republican Noise Machine: Right-Wing Media and How It Corrupts Democracy*. Crown Publishers.

2. Klaas, B. (2016). *The Despot's Accomplice: How the West Is Aiding and Abetting the Decline of Democracy*. Oxford University Press.

3. Pew Research Center. (Mar. 23, 2021). *Large Majorities of Newsmax and OAN News Consumers Also Go to Fox News*.

4. Rhodes, B. (2021). *After the Fall: Being American in the World We've Made*. Random House.

5. Bipartisan Policy Center. (2023). *How Did We Get Here: Primaries, Polarization, and Party Control*. https://bipartisanpolicy.org

6. Kustov, A., LaGatta, T., & Myagkov, M. (2021). *The Rise of Safe Seats and Party Indiscipline in the U.S. Congress*. Jackson Institute for Global Affairs, Yale University.

7. Reclaim the American Dream. (Jan. 18, 2022). *Voters Shut Out by Gerrymander Wars*. https://reclaimtheamericandream.org

8. Georgetown Institute for the Study of Markets and Ethics. (Mar. 15, 2023). *The Impact of Voter Turnout on Polarization*. https://marketsandethics.georgetown.edu

9. Stanford Institute for Economic Policy Research. (2023). *Want to Reduce Polarization in Congress? Make Moderates a Better Job Offer*. https://siepr.stanford.edu

10. Grose, C. R. (2020). "Reducing Legislative Polarization: Top-Two and Open Primaries Are Associated with More Moderate Legislators." *Journal of Political Institutions and Political Economy*, vol. 1, no. 1, pp. 1–22. https://doi.org/10.1086/711289

11. Klein, E. (2020). *Why We're Polarized*. Avid Reader Press / Simon & Schuster.

12. Rosenwald, B. (2019). *Talk Radio's America: How an Industry Took Over a Political Party That Took Over the United States*. Harvard University Press.

13. Fisher, M. (2022). *The Chaos Machine: The Inside Story of How Social Media Rewired Our Minds and Our World*. Little, Brown and Company.

14. Ben-Ghiat, R. (2020). *Strongmen: Mussolini to the Present.* W. W. Norton & Company.

15. American Bar Association. (2024). *Political Reforms to Combat Extremism.* https://www.americanbar.org

Chapter 14: The Power of Critical Thinking

1. Sagan, C. (1997). *The Demon-Haunted World: Science as a Candle in the Dark.* Ballantine Books.

2. Kahne, J., & Bowyer, B. (2017). "Educating for Democracy in a Digital Age: Media Literacy and the Challenge of Fake News." *American Educational Research Journal,* vol. 54, no. 3, pp. 399–441. https://doi.org/10.3102/0002831216679817

3. Pennycook, G., & Rand, D. G. (2019). "Lazy, Not Biased: Susceptibility to Partisan Fake News Is Better Explained by Lack of Reasoning Than by Motivated Reasoning." *Cognition,* vol. 188, pp. 39–50. https://doi.org/10.1016/j.cognition.2018.06.011

4. Levitin, D. J. (2016). *A Field Guide to Lies: Critical Thinking in the Information Age.* Dutton.

5. Cook, J., & Lewandowsky, S. (2011). *The Debunking Handbook.* University of Queensland Press. https://skepticalscience.com/docs/Debunking_Handbook.pdf

6. Tversky, A., & Kahneman, D. (1981). "The Framing of Decisions and the Psychology of Choice." *Science,* vol. 211, no. 4481, pp. 453–458. https://doi.org/10.1126/science.7455683

7. Wineburg, S., & McGrew, S. (2017). "Lateral Reading: Reading Less and Learning More When Evaluating Digital Information." Stanford History Education Group.

Chapter 15: Encouraging Media Literacy

1. Hobbs, R. (2020). *Mind Over Media: Propaganda Education for a Digital Age.* W. W. Norton & Company.

2. Postman, N. (1985). *Amusing Ourselves to Death: Public Discourse in the Age of Show Business.* Viking Penguin.

3. Civil. (2020). *The Civil Journalism Platform.* https://www.civil.co

4. Po.et. "Timestamping Digital Content on the Blockchain." https://po.et

5. PUBLIQ. "Decentralized Publishing Platform." https://publiq.network

6. NewsGuard. "News Reliability Ratings for Digital Content." https://www.newsguardtech.com

7. AdVerif.ai. "Automated Detection of Fake News and Inappropriate Content." https://www.adverif.ai

8. Google. *Fact Check Explorer.* https://toolbox.google.com/factcheck/explorer

9. Ovadya, A. (Mar. 2018). "The Infocalypse Is Coming. Are We Ready?" *The Atlantic.*

10. Sunstein, C. R. (2001). *#Republic: Divided Democracy in the Age of Social Media.* Princeton University Press.

11. Ressa, M. (Dec. 10, 2021). *Nobel Peace Prize Lecture.* Nobel Prize Committee.

Chapter 16: How to Have Conversations with Those Trapped in Misinformation

1. Sharot, T. (2017). *The Influential Mind: What the Brain Reveals About Our Power to Change Others.* Henry Holt and Co.

2. Nyhan, B., & Reifler, J. (2010). "When Corrections Fail: The Persistence of Political Misperceptions." *Political Behavior*, vol. 32, no. 2, pp. 303–330. https://doi.org/10.1007/s11109-010-9112-2

3. Boghossian, P., & Lindsay, J. (2019). *How to Have Impossible Conversations: A Very Practical Guide*. Lifelong Books.

4. Grant, A. (2021). *Think Again: The Power of Knowing What You Don't Know*. Viking.

5. Klein, E. (2020). *Why We're Polarized*. Avid Reader Press / Simon & Schuster.

Chapter 17: The Role of Education and Fact-Based Discourse in Saving Democracy

1. Brookings Institution. (2020). *Misinformation Is Eroding the Public's Confidence in Democracy*.

2. National Assessment of Educational Progress. (2022). *Eighth-Grade Scores Decline in Civics and U.S. History on the Nation's Report Card*. https://www.nationsreportcard.gov

3. Westheimer, J. (2015). *What Kind of Citizen? Educating Our Children for the Common Good*. Teachers College Press.

4. *Nature*. (2024). "Misinformation Poses a Bigger Threat to Democracy Than You Might Think." *Nature*.

5. Kovach, B., & Rosenstiel, T. (2014). *The Elements of Journalism: What Newspeople Should Know and the Public Should Expect*. Crown Publishing.

6. New America. (2020). *The Problem of Misinformation in a Democracy*. https://www.newamerica.org

7. Wardle, C., & Derakhshan, H. (2017). *Information Disorder: Toward an Interdisciplinary Framework for Research and Policymaking*. Council of Europe. https://rm.coe.int/information-disorder-report/1680764666

8. Froomkin, D. (n.d.) *Press Think*. https://presswatchers.org

Afterword

1. Arendt, H. (1973) *The Origins of Totalitarianism*. Harcourt, Brace & World, p. 474.

2. CBS News. (May 1, 2025). "Trump Sets Executive Order Record in His First 100 Days.".

3. Federal News Network. (Jan. 2025). "Trump Uses Mass Firing to Remove Independent Inspectors General at a Series of Agencies."

4. NPR. (Jan. 25, 2025). "Trump Fires Independent Inspectors General at Several Agencies."

5. Obama, B. (Apr. 21, 2022). "Remarks by President Obama on Disinformation and the Challenges to Democracy." Stanford University Cyber Policy Center.

6. Reuters. (May 2, 2025). "U.S. Supreme Court Justice Jackson Criticizes Trump's Attacks on Judges.".

7. Reuters. (May 8, 2025). "Trump Asks Supreme Court to Allow Him to End Humanitarian Parole for 500,000 People from Four Countries.".

8. Roberts, J. (May 8, 2025). "Chief Justice John Roberts Claps Back at MAGA Calls to Impeach 'Crooked' Judges." *The Daily Beast*.

9. The 19th News. (Apr. 17, 2025). "Supreme Court Sets Date in May to Hear Arguments on Trump's Birthright Citizenship Order."

10. The Guardian. (Jan. 28, 2025). "Trump Condemned Over 'Blatantly Illegal' Firings of Watchdog Chiefs."

11. The Guardian. (Mar. 23, 2025). "Trump's Defiance of Court Orders Is 'Testing the Fences' of the Rule of Law."

12. The White House. (Jan. 2025). *Ending Radical Indoctrination in K–12 Schooling.*

13. The White House. (Jan. 2025). *Granting Pardons and Commutation of Sentences for Certain Offenses Relating to the Events at or Near the United States Capitol on January 6, 2021.*

14. The White House. (Jan. 2025). *Establishing and Implementing the President's Department of Government Efficiency.*

15. The White House. (Mar. 2025). *Fact Sheet: President Donald J. Trump Removes DEI from the Federal Government.*

16. Bulletin of the Atomic Scientists. (2025). *Doomsday Clock Statement.*

Bibliography

1. **American Carnage: On the Front Lines of the Republican Civil War and the Rise of President Trump**
    Author: Tim Alberta
    Publisher: Harper
    Publication Date: July 16, 2019
    ISBN: 978-0062896445

2. **American Psychosis: A Historical Investigation of How the Republican Party Went Crazy**
    Author: David Corn
    Publisher: Twelve
    Publication Date: September 12, 2023
    ISBN: 978-1538723067

3. **Amusing Ourselves to Death: Public Discourse in the Age of Show Business**
    Author: Neil Postman
    Publisher: Penguin Books
    Publication Date: December 27, 2005
    ISBN: 978-0143036531

4. **Attack from Within: How Disinformation Is Sabotaging Democracy**
    Author: Barbara McQuade
    Publisher: Seven Stories Press
    Publication Date: February 27, 2024
    ISBN: 978-1644213636

5. **The Chaos Machine: The Inside Story of How Social Media Rewired Our Minds and Our World**
    Author: Max Fisher
    Publisher: Little, Brown and Company

Publication Date: September 6, 2022
ISBN: 978-0316703310

6. **Conspiracy: Why the Rational Believe the Irrational**
   Author: Michael Shermer
   Publisher: Johns Hopkins University Press
   Publication Date: February 7, 2024
   ISBN: 978-1421449074

7. **The Constitution of Knowledge: A Defense of Truth**
   Author: Jonathan Rauch
   Publisher: Brookings Institution Press
   Publication Date: June 22, 2021
   ISBN: 978-0815738879

8. **The Cult of Trump: A Leading Cult Expert Explains How the President Uses Mind Control**
   Author: Steven Hassan
   Publisher: Free Press
   Publication Date: September 1, 2020
   ISBN: 978-1982127343

9. **The Death of Expertise: The Campaign Against Established Knowledge and Why It Matters**
   Author: Tom Nichols
   Publisher: Oxford University Press
   Publication Date: April 3, 2024 (2nd edition)
   ISBN: 978-0190469412

10. **The Death of Truth: How Social Media and the Internet Gave Snake Oil Salesmen and Demagogues the Weapons They Needed to Destroy Trust and Polarize the World--And What We Can Do**
    Author: Steven Brill
    Publisher: Knopf

Publication Date: June 4, 2024
ISBN: 978-0525658313

11. **The Death of Truth: Notes on Falsehood in the Age of Trump**
Author: Michiko Kakutani
Publisher: William Collins
Publication Date: August 22, 2019
ISBN: 978-0008312800

12. **Demagogue for President: The Rhetorical Genius of Donald Trump**
Author: Jennifer Mercieca
Publisher: Texas A&M University Press
Publication Date: July 7, 2020
ISBN: 978-1623499068

13. **Don't Think of an Elephant!: Know Your Values and Frame the Debate**
Author: George Lakoff
Publisher: Chelsea Green
Publication Date: September 16, 2014
ISBN: 978-1603585941
The Echo Machine: How Right-Wing Extremism Created a Post-Truth America
Author: David Pakman
Publisher: Beacon Press
Publication Date: March 25, 2025
ISBN: 978-0807016534

14. **The Elements of Journalism, Revised and Updated 4th Edition: What Newspeople Should Know and the Public Should Expect**
Author: Bill Kovach and Tom Rosenstiel
Publisher: Crown
Publication Date: August 10, 2021
ISBN: 978-0593239353

15. **A Field Guide to Lies: Critical Thinking with Statistics and the Scientific Method**
Author: Daniel J. Levitin
Publisher: Dutton
Publication Date: November 19, 2019
ISBN: 978-0593182512

16. **The Filter Bubble: How the New Personalized Web Is Changing What We Read and How We Think**
Author: Eli Pariser
Publisher: Penguin Books
Publication Date: April 24, 2012
ISBN: 978-0143121237

17. **A Firehose of Falsehood: The Story of Disinformation**
Author: Teri Kanefield
Publisher: First Second Books
Publication Date: February 13, 2024
ISBN: 978-1250790439

18. **Foolproof: Why We Fall for Misinformation and How to Build Immunity**
Author: Sander van der Linden
Publisher: Generic
Publication Date: February 25, 2023
ASIN: B0BXDLLJ3R

19. **Hoax: Donald Trump, Fox News, and the Dangerous Distortion of Truth**
Author: Brian Stelter
Publisher: Atria/One Signal Publishers
Publication Date: August 25, 2020
ISBN: 978-1982142445

20. **How Democracies Die**
Authors: Steven Levitsky and Daniel Ziblatt
Publisher: Crown

Publication Date: January 8, 2019 (reprint edition)
ISBN: 978-1524762940

21. **How Fascism Works: The Politics of Us and Them**
Author: Jason Stanley
Publisher: Random House Trade Paperbacks
Publication Date: May 28, 2019
ISBN: 978-0525511854

22. **How Partisan Media Polarize America (Chicago Studies in American Politics)**
Author: Matthew Levendusky
Publisher: University of Chicago Press
Publication Date: September 3, 2013
ISBN: 978-0226069012

23. **How to Have Impossible Conversations: A Very Practical Guide**
Author: Peter Boghossian and James Lindsay
Publisher: Balance
Publication Date: September 17, 2019
ISBN: 978-0738285320

24. **How to Stand Up to a Dictator**
Author: Maria Ressa
Publisher: Harper
Publication Date: November 29, 2022
ISBN: 978-0063257511

25. **Ignorance: A Global History**
Author: Peter Burke
Publisher: Yale University Press
Publication Date: April 30, 2024
ISBN: 978-0300276503

26. **Ignorance and Bliss: On Wanting Not to Know**
Author: Mark Lilla
Publisher: Farrar, Straus, and Giroux
Publication Date: December 3, 2024
ISBN: 978-0374174354

27. **It Was All a Lie: How the Republican Party Became Donald Trump**
Author: Stuart Stevens
Publisher: Knopf
Publication Date: August 4, 2020
ISBN: 978-0525658450

28. **Lie Machines: How to Save Democracy from Troll Armies, Deceitful Robots, Junk News Operations, and Political Operatives**
Author: Philip N. Howard
Publisher: Yale University Press
Publication Date: May 19, 2020
ISBN: 978-0300250206

29. **A Lot of People Are Saying: The New Conspiracism and the Assault on Democracy**
Author: Nancy L. Rosenblum and Russell Muirhead
Publisher: Princeton University Press
Publication Date: May 21, 2019
ISBN: 978-0691188836

30. **Ministry of Truth: Democracy, Reality, and the Republicans' War on the Recent Past**
Authors: Steve Benen
Publisher: Mariner Books
Publication Date: August 13, 2024
ISBN: 978-0063393677

31. **The Misinformation Age: How False Beliefs Spread**
Authors: Cailin O'Connor and James Owen Weatherall
Publisher: Yale University Press
Publication Date: February 18, 2020
ISBN: 978-0274758531

32. **Money, Lies, and God: Inside the Movement to Destroy American Democracy**
Author: Katherine Stewart
Publisher: Bloomsbury Publishing

Publication Date: February 18, 2025
ISBN: 978-1635578546

33. **Network of Lies: The Epic Saga of Fox News, Donald Trump, and the Battle for American Democracy**
Author: Brian Stelter
Publisher: Atria/One Signal Publishers
Publication Date: November 14, 2023
ISBN: 978-1668046906

34. **Network Propaganda: Manipulation, Disinformation, and Radicalization in American Politics**
Author: Yochal Benkler, Robert Faris, Hal Roberts
Publisher: Oxford University Press
Publication Date: October 15, 2018
ISBN: 978-0190923631

35. **News Deserts and Ghost Newspapers: Will Local News Survive?**
Author: Penelope Muse Abernathy
Publisher: UNC Ctr Innovation and Sustainability Local Media
Publication Date: September 15, 2020
ISBN: 978-1469661308

36. **Nothing Is True and Everything Is Possible: The Surreal Heart of the New Russia**
Author: Peter Pomerantsev
Publisher: PublicAffairs (reprint edition)
Publication Date: November 10, 2015
ISBN: 978-1610396004

37. **A Passion for Ignorance: What we Choose Not to Know and Why**
Author: Renata Salecl
Publisher: Princeton University Press
Publication Date: November 9, 2022
ISBN: 978-0691240992

38. **The Persuaders: At the Front Lines of the Fight for Hearts, Minds, and Democracy**
Author: Anand Giridharadas
Publisher: Knopf
Publication Date: October 18, 2022
ISBN: 978-0593318997

39. **The Political Mind: A Cognitive Scientist's Guide to Your Brain and Its Politics**
Author: George Lakoff
Publisher: Penguin Publishing Group
Publication Date: June 2, 2009
ISBN: 978-0143115687

40. **Post-Truth**
Author: Lee McIntyre
Publisher: The MIT Press
Publication Date: February 16, 2018
ISBN: 978-0262535045

41. **Profiles in Ignorance: How America's Politicians Got Dumb and Dumber**
Author: Andy Borowitz
Publisher: Avid Reader Press / Simon & Schuster
Publication Date: September 5, 2023
ISBN: 978-1668003893

42. **The Psychology of Conspiracy Theories (The Psychology of Everything)**
Author: Jan-Willem van Prooijen
Publisher: Routledge
Publication Date: March 15, 2018
ISBN: 978-1138696105

43. **#Republic: Divided Democracy in the Age of Social Media**
Author: Cass R. Sunstein
Publisher: Princeton University Press
Publication Date: March 14, 2017
ISBN: 978-0691175515

44. **Republic of Lies: American Conspiracy Theorists and Their Surprising Rise to Power**
Author: Anna Merlan
Publisher: Metropolitan Books (reprint edition)
Publication Date: July 14, 2020
ISBN: 978-1250231277

45. **The Republican Noise Machine: Right-Wing Media and How It Corrupts Democracy**
Author: David Brock
Publisher: Crown
Publication Date: May 18, 2004
ISBN: 978-1400048755

46. **The Righteous Mind: Why Good People Are Divided by Politics and Religion**
Author: Jonathan Haidt
Publisher: Vintage
Publication Date: February 12, 2013
ISBN: 978-0307455772

47. **Stolen Focus: Why You Can't Pay Attention—and How to Think Deeply Again**
Author: Johan Hari
Publisher: Crown Publishing Group
Publication Date: January 25, 2022
ISBN: 978-0593138519

48. **Strangers in Their Own Land: Anger and Mourning on the American Right**
Author: Arlie Russell Hochschild
Publisher: The New Press
Publication Date: September 6, 2016
ISBN: 978-1620972250

49. **Think Again: The Power of Knowing What You Don't Know**
Author: Adam Grant
Publisher: Penguin Books

Publication Date: December 26, 2023
ISBN: 978-1984878120

50. **This Is Not Propaganda: Adventures in the War Against Reality**
Author: Peter Pomerantsev
Publisher: Faber & Faber
Publication Date: October 1, 2020
ISBN: 978-0571338641

51. **Truth Decay: An Initial Exploration of the Diminishing Role of Facts and Analysis in American Public Life**
Authors: Jennifer Kavanagh and Michael D. Rich
Publisher: RAND Corporation
Publication Date: January 26, 2018
ISBN: 978-0833099945

52. **Twilight of Democracy: The Seductive Lure of Authoritarianism**
Author: Anne Applebaum
Publisher: Vintage
Publication Date: June 22, 2021
ISBN: 978-1984899507

53. **Why We're Polarized**
Author: Ezra Klein
Publisher: Avid Reader Press
Publication Date: June 15, 2021
ISBN: 978-1476700366

54. **Willful Ignorance and Stupid Political Decisions: The 2024 Election and How to Combat the Rise of Oligarchy in America**
Author: J. Dan Rothwell
Publisher: And So It Begins Books
Publication Date: March 19, 2025
ISBN: 978-8992909609

55. **Wrong: How Media, Politics, and Identity Drive Our Appetite for Misinformation**
Author: Dannagal Goldthwaite Young
Publisher: Johns Hopkins University Press
Publication Date: October 17, 2023
ISBN: 978-1421447759

Historical Quotes

Isaac Asimov

"Anti-intellectualism has been a constant thread winding its way through our political and cultural life, nurtured by the false notion that democracy means the 'my ignorance is just as good as your knowledge.'"

Marcus Aurelius

"It's the truth I'm after and the truth never harmed anyone. What harms us is to persist in self-deceit and ignorance."

Jacques Ellul

"Naturally, the educated man does not believe in propaganda; he shrugs and is convinced that propaganda has no effect on him. This is, in fact, one of his great weaknesses."

Erich Fromm

"That millions of people share the same forms of mental pathology does not make these people sane."

Stephen Fry

"The only reason people do not know much is because they do not care to know. They are incurious. Incuriosity is the oddest and most foolish failing there is."

Jürgen Habermas	"A post-truth democracy … would no longer be a democracy."
Aldous Huxley	"Reality cannot be ignored except at a price; and the longer the ignorance is persisted in, the higher and more terrible becomes the price that must be paid."
Dresden James	"When a well-packaged web of lies has been sold gradually to the masses over generations, the truth will seem utterly preposterous and its speaker a raving lunatic."
Franz Kafka	"No matter how much you keep encouraging someone who is blindfolded to stare through the cloth, he still won't see a thing."
Immanuel Kant	"If the truth shall kill them, let them die."
Soren Kierkegaard	"A fire broke out backstage in a theatre. The clown came out to warn the public; they thought it was a joke and applauded. He repeated it; the acclaim was even greater. I think that's just how the world will come to an end: To the general applause of wits who believe it's a joke."

Gerald Massey	"They must find it difficult, those who have taken authority as truth, rather than truth as authority."
Friedrich Nietzsche	"Sometimes people don't want to hear the truth because they don't want their illusions destroyed."
George Orwell	"The most effective way to destroy people is to deny and obliterate their own understanding of their history."
George Orwell	"It's frightful that people who are so ignorant have so much influence."
George Orwell	"However much you deny the truth, the truth goes on existing."
George Orwell	"In the end the Party would announce that two and two made five, and you would have to believe it. It was inevitable that they should make that claim sooner or later: the logic of their position demanded it … The Party told you to reject the evidence of your eyes and ears. It was their final, most essential command."
Plato	"Ignorance is the root and stem of all evil."

Bill Richardson

"Ignorance has always been the weapon of tyrants; enlightenment the salvation of the free."

Maximilien Robespierre

"The secret of freedom lies in educating people, whereas the secret of tyranny is in keeping them ignorant."

Carl Sagan

"One of the saddest lessons of history is this: If we've been bamboozled long enough, we tend to reject any evidence of the bamboozle. We're no longer interested in finding out the truth. The bamboozle has captured us. It's simply too painful to acknowledge, even to ourselves, that we've been taken. Once you give a charlatan power over you, you almost never get it back."

George Bernard Shaw

"Beware of false knowledge; it is more dangerous than ignorance."

Edward Snowden

"People don't realize how hard it is to speak the truth, to a world full of people who don't realize they are living a lie."

Aleksandr Solzhenitsyn

"The simple step of a courageous individual is not to take part in the lie."

Thomas Sowell "It is usually futile to try to talk facts and analysis to people who are enjoying a sense of moral superiority in their ignorance."

Thomas Sowell "Some things are believed because they are demonstrably true, but many other things are believed simply because they have been asserted repeatedly, and repetition has been accepted as a substitute for evidence."

David Stevens "The truth is still the truth, even if no one believes it. A lie is still a lie, even if everyone believes it."

TruthTheory "I miss the old days when logic and facts were more important than feelings and delusions."

TruthTheory "Whenever I'm feeling down, I just remind myself that a trillion dollar's-worth of propaganda didn't work on me."

Mark Twain "It's easier to fool people than to convince them that they have been fooled."

Neil deGrasse Tyson "I know of no time in human history where ignorance was better than knowledge."

Neil deGrasse Tyson	"If your *personal beliefs* deny what's objectively true about the world, then they're more accurately called *personal delusions*."
Unknown	"We are witnessing the twisted ugly fruit of 20+ years of Fox News weaponizing ignorance and hatred."
Unknown	"The simple fact that you were fooled and conned doesn't make you an idiot. What makes you an idiot is when you blatantly refuse to look at the truth and make the conscious decision to believe the lies."
Swami Vivekananda	"Who makes us ignorant? We ourselves. We put our hands over our eyes and weep that it is dark."
Voltaire	"It is difficult to free fools from the chains they revere."
George Washington	"If freedom of speech is taken away, then dumb and silent we may be led, like sheep, to the slaughter."

Index

Index

About the Author

Stephen M. Fry, Ph.D. has had a varied career spanning physics, engineering, consulting, corporate management, and venture capital—as well as writing. He earned a Ph.D. in Quantum Electronics from UCLA, along with an M.S. in Electrical Engineering, and B.S. in Physics (also from UCLA), and an M.B.A. in Financial Analysis from National University. He has published extensively, including dozens of technical papers and presentations, and is the author or co-author of nine books on medical technology. *Weaponization of Ignorance* reflects his more recent focus—a decade of reading, research, and reflection on how media, psychology, and culture shape political belief. He lives in El Dorado Hills, California with his wife, and their border collie.

www.ingramcontent.com/pod-product-compliance
Lightning Source LLC
Chambersburg PA
CBHW060453290526
45791CB00001B/91